impact

2

SERIES EDITORS
JoAnn (Jodi) Crandall
Joan Kang Shin

AUTHOR
Katherine Stannett

NATIONAL GEOGRAPHIC LEARNING | CENGAGE Learning

Australia • Brazil • Mexico • Singapore • United Kingdom • United States

Thank you to the educators who provided invaluable feedback during the development of *Impact*:

EXPERT PANEL

Márcia Ferreira, Academic Coordinator, CCBEU, Franca, Brazil

Jianwei Song, Vice-general Manager, Ensure International Education, Harbin, China

María Eugenia Flores, Academic Director, and **Liana Rojas-Binda**, Head of Recruitment & Training, Centro Cultural Costarricense-Norteamericano, San José, Costa Rica

Liani Setiawati, M.Pd., SMPK 1 BPK PENABUR Bandung, Bandung, Indonesia

Micaela Fernandes, Head of Research and Development Committee and Assessment Committee, Pui Ching Middle School, Macau

Héctor Sánchez Lozano, Academic Director, and **Carolina Tripodi**, Head of the Juniors Program, Proulex, Guadalajara, Mexico

Rosario Giraldez, Academic Director, Alianza Cultural, Montevideo, Uruguay

REVIEWERS

BRAZIL

Renata Cardoso, Colégio do Sol, Guara, DF

Fábio Delano Vidal Carneiro, Colégio Sete de Setembro, Fortaleza

Cristiano Carvalho, Centro Educacional Leonardo da Vinci, Vitória

Silvia Corrêa, Associação Alumni, São Paulo

Carol Espinosa, Associação Cultural Brasil Estados Unidos, Salvador

Marcia Ferreira, Centro Cultural Brasil Estados Unidos, Franca

Clara Haddad, ELT Consultant, São Paulo

Elaine Carvalho Chaves Hodgson, Colégio Militar de Brasília, Brasília

Thays Farias Galvão Ladosky, Associação Brasil América, Recife

Itana Lins, Colégio Anchieta, Salvador

Samantha Mascarenhas, Associação Cultural Brasil Estados Unidos, Salvador

Ann Marie Moreira, Pan American School of Bahia, Bahia

Rodrigo Ramirez, CEETEPS- Fatec Zona Sul, São Paulo

Paulo Torres, Vitória Municipality, Vitória

Renata Zainotte, Go Up Idiomas, Rio de Janeiro

CHINA

Zhou Chao, MaxEn Education, Beijing

Zhu Haojun, Only International Education, Shanghai

Su Jing, Beijing Chengxun International English School, Beijing

Jianjun Shen, Phoenix City International School, Guangzhou

COSTA RICA

Luis Antonio Quesada-Umaña, Centro Cultural Costarricense Norteamericano, San José

INDONESIA

Luz S. Ismail, M.A., LIA Institute of Language and Vocational Training, Jakarta

Selestin Zainuddin, LIA Institute of Language and Vocational Training, Jakarta

Rosalia Dian Devitasari, SMP Kolese Kanisius, Jakarta

JAPAN

John Williams, Tezukayama Gakuen, Nara

MEXICO

Nefertiti González, Instituto Mexicano Madero, Puebla

Eugenia Islas, Instituto Tlalpan, Mexico City

Marta MM Seguí, Colegio Velmont A.C., Puebla

SOUTH KOREA

Min Yuol (Alvin) Cho, Global Leader English Education, Yong In

THAILAND

Panitnan Kalayanapong, Eduzone Co., Ltd., Bangkok

TURKEY

Damla Çaltuğ, İELEV, Istanbul

Basak Nalcakar Demiralp, Ankara Sinav College, Ankara

Humeyra Olcayli, İstanbul Bilim College, Istanbul

VIETNAM

Chantal Kruger, ILA Vietnam, Hô Chí Minh

Ai Nguyen Huynh, Vietnam USA Society, Hô Chí Minh

impact

2

Unit 1

ANNIE GRIFFITHS **Photographer**

Annie Griffiths was one of the first women photographers for *National Geographic*. She fell in love with photography when she took a class in college. She has worked in more than 100 countries taking colorful pictures of people and places.

Unit 2

PARDIS SABETI **Computational Geneticist**

Pardis Sabeti was born in Tehran, Iran. She is the lead singer and bass player in a rock band. She's also a computational geneticist. Pardis works to understand and control dangerous diseases like Ebola. She wants to keep the world healthy, and she knows that, in order to do that, people need to work together. They need to share information, understand other people, and have fun!

Unit 3

AMBER CASE **Cyborg Anthropologist**

How do humans and technology interact? Amber Case is on a mission to find out. As a cyborg anthropologist, she studies the relationship between people and technology. Amber looks at how the use of gadgets and computers affects our lives in both positive and negative ways. How does technology affect your life?

Unit 4

KATY CROFF BELL **Oceanographer**

Katy Croff Bell is an underwater detective! As an oceanographer, Katy uses deep-sea technology to explore the ocean. She spends much of her time aboard the E/V *Nautilus* as it travels the world's seas. She's excited to share her work with the rest of us using *telepresence* technology. With this technology, we can use computers to explore with Katy as she makes discoveries on the ocean floor.

Unit 5

KEVIN HAND **Planetary Scientist/Astrobiologist**

Kevin Hand knows that life can thrive in the most extreme environments. Kevin works at the NASA Jet Propulsion Laboratory as a planetary scientist and astrobiologist. He researches one of Jupiter's moons, Europa. Its deep oceans may be the perfect environment for microscopic extremophiles. Kevin thinks studying Europa may be our best chance at finding life beyond Earth!

Unit 6

TRISTRAM STUART **Author/Campaigner**

Want to know something shocking? People waste more than one-third of the food that's produced! Tristram Stuart, an author and campaigner, is trying to change that. He raises awareness of food waste by holding public feasts and disco parties. Tristram believes everyone can be less wasteful by taking only what they need.

Unit 7

SHANNON GALPIN **Adventurer/Humanitarian**

Shannon Galpin thinks art isn't just for private galleries. Shannon wants art in public spaces where everyone can enjoy it. She organized a free public art show in Afghanistan, in which she displayed life-size photos of daily scenes from Afghan culture. This was the first time some Afghan people got to see the beauty and culture of different parts of their country.

Unit 8

JIMMY CHIN **Climber/Photographer**

Avalanches, steep cliffs, and below-freezing temperatures? It's all in a day's work for climber, filmmaker, and photographer, Jimmy Chin. Jimmy goes on four or five expeditions each year. He thinks his most important job on the expedition is to first be a safe, reliable member of the team—taking pictures is second. But he's willing to take risks to get the perfect shot. Jimmy's love of exploring keeps him going. He thinks the human spirit is strong enough to overcome any obstacle.

Color Matters

"When multiple colors dance across the same scene, the result can be a carnival."

—Annie Griffiths

People celebrating Carnaval in Rio de Janeiro, Brazil

1. Name all of the different colors that you see in the photo. Which is your favorite?

2. Would you like to be at the place in the photo? Why or why not?

3. Imagine this photo in black and white. What would you think of it? What would be lost?

9

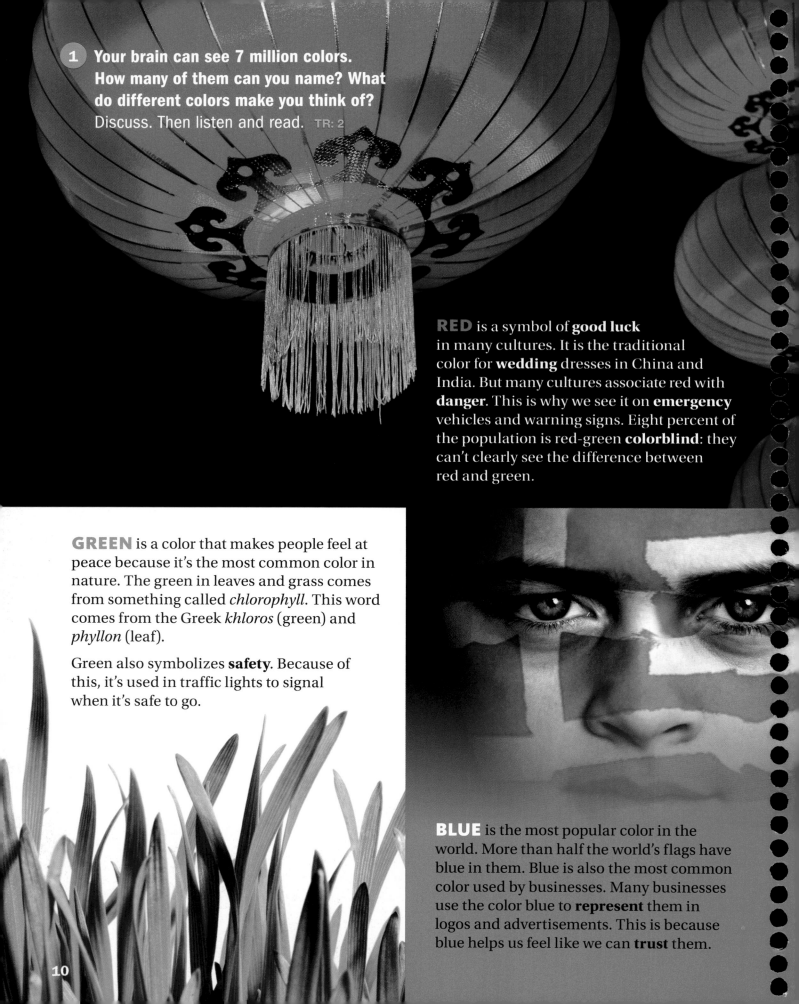

RED is a symbol of **good luck** in many cultures. It is the traditional color for **wedding** dresses in China and India. But many cultures associate red with **danger**. This is why we see it on **emergency** vehicles and warning signs. Eight percent of the population is red-green **colorblind**: they can't clearly see the difference between red and green.

GREEN is a color that makes people feel at peace because it's the most common color in nature. The green in leaves and grass comes from something called *chlorophyll*. This word comes from the Greek *khloros* (green) and *phyllon* (leaf).

Green also symbolizes **safety**. Because of this, it's used in traffic lights to signal when it's safe to go.

BLUE is the most popular color in the world. More than half the world's flags have blue in them. Blue is also the most common color used by businesses. Many businesses use the color blue to **represent** them in logos and advertisements. This is because blue helps us feel like we can **trust** them.

ORANGE gets its name from the fruit. The word originally described the taste of the fruit's peel, but by the sixteenth century, *orange* was also the name of this **bright** color.

YELLOW is the color of taxis and school buses because it's the most **visible** color on the road. Like red, yellow is also used to **warn** people of dangerous situations. Because it attracts attention, yellow is used for highlighter pens. The bright color activates different parts of the brain that help the reader remember the highlighted text.

INDIGO is a dark color between blue and purple. Indigo clothing was a sign of luxury in the past because indigo **dye** came from a rare plant. It was very expensive, and few people could wear clothes made with this dye. Now we use indigo dye to make blue jeans.

VIOLET is a **light** purple color. It is one of the oldest colors in the world. There are violet cave paintings in France that are 25,000 years old! However, in some countries, for example Thailand and Brazil, violet is the color of **death**.

2 **Learn new words.** Listen and repeat. TR: 3

3 **Work in pairs.** Which colors make you feel happy? Sad?

4 **Read and write the words from the list.** Make any necessary changes.

bright	danger	light	represent
safety	visible	warn	wedding

Photographer Annie Griffiths has traveled all around the world. In many of the places she's visited, Annie has seen _____ . However, Annie chooses to focus on the beauty of the places and the people she meets. This photo is one of her favorites. It shows her son resting next to her friend. She took it after a _____ celebration in Jordan. For Annie, the photograph expresses her son's feeling of _____ and happiness.

Annie loves to use _____ colors in her photos. She says, "It's difficult to photograph a very dark thing, for example the black fur of a panther, or a very _____ thing, for example a snowy field. But one spot of color in a picture can make it look amazing."

5 **Learn new words.** Listen to these words and match them to the definitions. Then listen and repeat. TR: 4 and 5

common	flag	luxury	to signal

1. _____ give a sign or a warning
2. _____ happening often
3. _____ a special thing
4. _____ the symbol of a country

Photographer
Annie Griffiths

6 **Choose an activity.**

1. **Work independently.** Choose a favorite photograph, and show it to the class. Describe the photo, and talk about its colors. Explain why you like it so much.

2. **Work in pairs.** Discuss the saying: *A picture is worth a thousand words.* What do you think this means? Do you agree with it? Why or why not?

3. **Work in groups.** Your teacher asks you to paint your classroom. Which colors will you choose for the walls, ceiling, desks, and chairs? Why? Create a design suggestion together.

Correcting information

The sky is blue.	Actually, <u>it isn't blue</u>.
	As a matter of fact, <u>the light from the sun is lots of colors</u>.
	In fact, <u>we see blue because blue light rays are shorter than light rays of other colors</u>.
	After all, <u>the sky changes from blue to red when the sun sets in the evening</u>.

7 **Listen.** How do the speakers correct information? Write the words and phrases you hear. TR: 7

8 **Read and complete the dialogue.**

Jaime: White is the most popular color for wedding dresses.

Ana: _____ , it isn't a popular color everywhere.

Jaime: Really?

Ana: Yes. _____ , white is the color of death in China, Korea, and other Asian countries.

Jaime: Wow, I didn't know that.

Ana: _____ , red is the color of weddings and celebrations in India and China.

Jaime: Interesting! I think red is a great color for wedding dresses.

_____ , it is a symbol of love in many cultures!

9 **Work in pairs.** Place all of the cards on the desk with the photos facing up. Both students take cards with matching photos. One partner reads information, and the other corrects it.

Correct by saying:

A polar bear's fur isn't white. It's clear. It reflects the light and this makes it look white.

Go to p. 153.

Polar bears have white fur.

As a matter of fact, their fur isn't white. It's clear, but it reflects the light. This makes it look white.

10 **Work in groups.** When is it important to correct information? What do you need to consider when correcting what someone else says? How do the words and phrases above help you to communicate better?

Comparatives and superlatives: Comparing two or more things

Adjective	Comparative	Superlative
Purple is a **popular** color.	Green is **more popular than** purple.	Blue is **the most popular** color in the world.
Green peppers are **tasty**.	Red peppers are **tastier than** green peppers.	Yellow peppers are **the tastiest** peppers.
Red grapes are **good**.	Red grapes are **better than** green grapes.	Red grapes are **the best**.

11 **Read.** Choose the correct word or phrase to complete the paragraph.

hungrier	larger	most delicious	sweeter	worse

When you see your favorite food on a red plate, you probably feel hungry. But you feel

_____ when it's on a white plate. Why? Research shows that colors can

really affect our feelings about food. For example, when you add red dye to water, it tastes

_____ than normal water, as if you've added sugar. The food that you

think is the _____ will probably taste _____

to you if you change its color to blue. This is because blue is a very unnatural color for food.

Color can also affect how much we eat. In one experiment, people were asked

to serve themselves some pasta with white sauce. The people with red plates

took a small portion, while the people with white plates took a much

_____ portion. Can you guess why this happens?

12 **Read.** Complete the sentences with the correct comparative or superlative forms. Then listen and check your answers. TR: 9

1. Dark green vegetables are _____ (high/low) in vitamin C than light green vegetables.

2. Yellow bananas are _____ (salty/sweet) green bananas, but green bananas are _____ (good/bad) for you.

3. Blue is _____ (common/unusual) color for food.

4. _____ (healthy/popular) diet includes foods of many different colors.

13 **Work in pairs.** Make a list of your five favorite foods. Then share your list. Make comparisons about those foods.

> Apples are better for you than cookies, but cookies are sweeter!

14 **Learn new words.** Listen and read to find out about colors and moods. Then listen and repeat. **TR: 10 and 11**

We make strong **connections** between colors and feelings.

GREEN RELAXED

RED NERVOUS

BLUE DEPRESSED

15 **Work in pairs.** Discuss how you feel when you see these things.

I feel relaxed when I see green trees.

I feel nervous when I see red lights on a car.

Me, too! But I feel more relaxed when I look at blue artwork.

16 **Work in groups.** Compare your answers to Activity 15 with another pair. Then choose two other colors and say how they make you feel.

PURPLE POWER
THE HISTORY OF ONE OF THE MOST POPULAR COLORS

Purple is one of the most popular colors today. There are purple clothes, purple handbags, purple bicycles, purple furniture, even purple computers! But in the past, purple was a very expensive and unusual color.

Let's take a look at the rich and sometimes dangerous history of the color purple.

THE VERY BEGINNING

Some scientists believe that the first organisms to appear on Earth over 500 million years ago probably looked purple, not green. Plants today are green because they use green chlorophyll to produce energy. But these early organisms probably used something called *retinal*, which is a dark purple color.

17 **Before you read, discuss in pairs.** Look at the photos and the timeline. What do you think the reading is about?

18 **Learn new words.** Find these words in the text. Use the other words in the sentences to guess each word's meaning. Then listen and repeat. TR: 12

| company | to notice | ordinary | royalty |

19 **While you read, think about the order of the events.** TR: 13

20 **After you read, discuss in pairs.**

1. Why do scientists think that the earliest organisms were purple?

2. Why was the color purple so expensive during the Roman Empire?

3. Who usually wore purple in England in the sixteenth century?

4. How did William Perkin discover a way to make purple dye? What advantage did his discovery have?

3,000 YEARS AGO

During the time of the Roman Empire, it was very difficult to make purple dye. The dye came from sea snails. But 10,000 dead sea snails got you just one gram of purple dye . . . as well as a very bad smell! This special purple dye was called *Tyrian purple*, and it was the preferred color of emperors.

500 YEARS AGO

In sixteenth-century England, purple was only for royalty. Queen Elizabeth I's clothes were purple, but ordinary people were not allowed to wear the color.

150 YEARS AGO

In 1856, William Perkin, an 18-year-old science student, noticed something strange while conducting an experiment. The chemicals he used to clean his equipment combined with the chemicals he used in his experiment, and produced a bright purple color. This discovery led Perkin to start a company using this chemical combination to make purple dye. The dye was much cheaper than the sea-snail dye. Thanks to Perkin, now anyone can wear purple clothes.

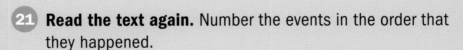

21 **Read the text again.** Number the events in the order that they happened.

_____ Only Queen Elizabeth I wears purple clothes.

_____ Sea snails are used to make purple clothes for emperors.

_____ Many of the Earth's plants appear to be purple, not green.

_____ Anyone can wear purple clothes.

_____ William Perkin discovers how to make purple dye.

22 **Discuss in groups.**

1. What color clothes do you like to wear? Why?

2. In Roman and Elizabethan times, purple was a sign of luxury. What color means luxury to you? Does the color purple have any special meaning in your culture?

3. Why do some people like to have luxury items, such as clothing? Are luxury items important to you? Why or why not?

VIDE▷

23 **Before you watch, discuss in pairs.** How do we use color in our life? Think about ways that color warns or informs us about things.

24 **Work in pairs.** You're going to watch a video called *Seeing Colors?* Look at the photo. How many different colors can you see? Do you think that all animals see colors the same as you do?

25 Watch scene 1.1. **While you watch, write the letter for each color in order, based on the range of visible light.**

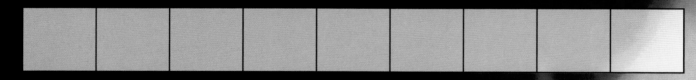

a. dark blue   b. green   c. infrared   d. light blue   e. orange   f. red   g. ultraviolet   h. violet   i. yellow

26 **After you watch, work in pairs to answer the questions.**

1. Why don't insects and animals see colors like most humans do?

2. What can bees see in flowers that is invisible to humans?

3. How can a snake see a mouse in the dark?

4. What color is infrared light to a snake?

5. What percentage of men are color-blind? What percentage of women are color-blind?

27 **Work in pairs.** Choose one of these gadgets, and find out how it uses infrared light. Share your answer with the class.

> TV remote control
>
> supermarket check-out scanner
>
> night-vision goggles
>
> car keys

A mouse visible in a *thermogram*, an image that shows an object's temperature

28 **Choose an activity.**

1. **Work independently.** Find pictures of things in nature that match each color in the range of visible light. Arrange the pictures in order on a sheet of paper, and glue them. Then label each item and its color.

2. **Work in pairs.** Go online to find out why you see a rainbow when it rains on a sunny day. Make a presentation to explain the science.

3. **Work in groups.** How important is color in your life? Can you imagine a life without color? What problems might there be? List at least three.

19

The: Identifying general and specific things

There's a coat in my closet. **The** coat is red.

The sun is shining in **the** sky.

People often feel depressed when they see **the** color black.

29 **Read.** Circle the correct word.

The / A Colors of Success

Imagine you're at a shopping mall. You want to go to _the / a_ café and get _the / a_ drink and _the / a_ snack. There are two different cafés in the mall. How do you choose _the / a_ café you want to visit? You probably look at the prices and the menus. But _the / a_ colors that _the / a_ café uses are also very important.

Do you want to feel calm and relaxed? Then you will probably choose The Coffee Place. _The / A_ green color makes you think of nature and peace.

Do you want to go someplace exciting and lively? Then you will probably choose The Coffee Machine. Many companies use _the / a_ color red because it seems bright and fun, and it attracts young people.

Think about your favorite brands. Which colors do they use? What do those colors mean to you?

30 **Work in pairs.** Take turns naming familiar brand-name products. Can your partner name the colors for the brand? Why do you think the companies chose the colors for each product?

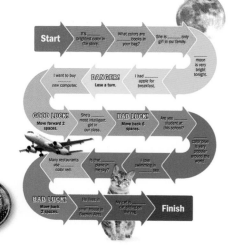

31 **Work in pairs.** Take turns. Use a coin to move. (Heads = 1 space; tails = 2 spaces) Complete each sentence with _the_ or _a / an_.

20

Go to p. 155.

WRITING

A topic sentence introduces the main idea of a paragraph. The topic sentence is usually the first sentence of the paragraph. It explains:

- why you are writing
- what you want to say

Look at these examples of topic sentences:

In this article, I'm going to discuss the history of the color orange.
When taking a photograph, it's important to think about light and color.

32 **Read the announcement and the response.** Underline the topic sentence.

COMPETITION

Write and tell us about your favorite color.

What color do you want to see at home and around town this season? Tell us what the color means to you.

I would like to tell you about my favorite color and explain why I think it's perfect for this season. My favorite color is orange. I think it's a warm and bright color, and it makes me feel happy and safe. When I see this color, I think of the fall. Although it gets cooler and the days are much shorter, I love the fall. When I go outside, I enjoy walking through the dark orange leaves and listening to the sound they make under my feet. I also think of the smell of fire when I see this color. It's great to be at home and sit by the warm fire with my family. Orange is also the color of my favorite food—pumpkin soup. It's so delicious! This warm and beautiful color should be everywhere this season—outside, in our homes, and even on our plates!

33 **Work in pairs.** Make a list of the things that the writer connects with his/her favorite color. Do you think his/her ideas are effective? Why or why not?

34 **Write.** Write a paragraph about your favorite color and what you associate with this color. Use a strong topic sentence.

Look for Opportunities

"Look around and ask yourself, 'Who needs pictures? Who needs help?' With photography, the opportunities are endless . . ."

—Annie Griffiths
National Geographic Photographer

1. **Watch scene 1.2.**

2. Discuss how photographers can use their skills to help other people.

3. Think about issues or social problems in your area. How could you use photographs to teach others about these issues?

Make an Impact

(A) Plan and create an art presentation.

- Research the use of color in Aboriginal art.

- Draw an object from your own culture using Aboriginal art techniques.

- Present your drawing to the class. Explain why you chose the colors you used.

(B) Plan and make a presentation about color and taste.

- Choose five foods. Use food coloring to change each food's color.

- Ask friends and family to taste and react to the foods.

- Present the results to the class.

(C) Blog about colors in your community.

- Find colorful people, places, and things in your community. Take photos of them.

- Write a blog about your photos. Explain why you took each photo and how the colors make you feel.

- Publish your blog and respond to your classmates' comments.

Feeling Good?

"Science brings people together, working toward a common cause—fighting disease."
—Pardis Sabeti

Girls on bikes in Mandalay, Myanmar

1. Look at the girls in the photo. How do you think they feel? Why do you think they feel this way?

2. How has science helped to improve people's health over the last 100 years? Give examples.

3. Work in small groups to think of three ways in which science affects your daily life. Share your ideas with the class.

How are you feeling today? Do you have a **sore** throat? Are you coughing? Sneezing? These are all very common **symptoms** that signal your body is fighting a **disease**. Your **immune system** works to protect you from diseases, but when it is weakened, you feel sick. The illness that you feel could be caused by one of two things: **bacteria** or **viruses**.

Bacteria are organisms with just one **cell**. They can survive outside the body, but we also have trillions of bacteria living in our bodies.

In fact, there are more bacteria than human cells in our bodies. But don't worry: ninety-nine percent of these bacteria are good for us. They allow us to feel positive emotions, **protect** us from disease, and help us **digest** food. Your mouth alone contains more bacteria than there are people on Earth! Unfortunately, there are also bad bacteria that cause illnesses. We can **treat** these bacterial **infections** with **antibiotics**.

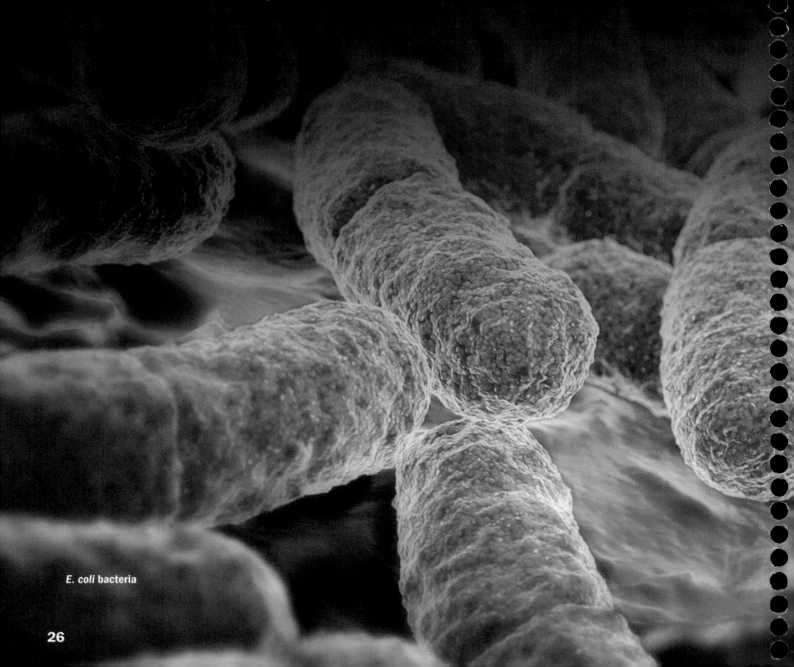

E. coli bacteria

Viruses are smaller than bacteria. They cannot exist without a host—an animal or plant to live in. That person next to you who's sneezing? She's the host of a virus. So, watch out! With each sneeze, she sends you over 100,000 virus cells, traveling at a speed of over 160 kph (100 mph)! Once those cells **invade** your body, you become the host. The virus then changes in order to make more viruses in your body. If you get a virus, you can't treat it with antibiotics. You simply need to wait until your body gets rid of it. Of course, you can protect yourself from viruses such as the flu by getting **vaccinations**, or even just by washing your hands. Over eighty percent of viruses are spread by touching an infected person or thing, so be sure to take care of yourself and stay healthy!

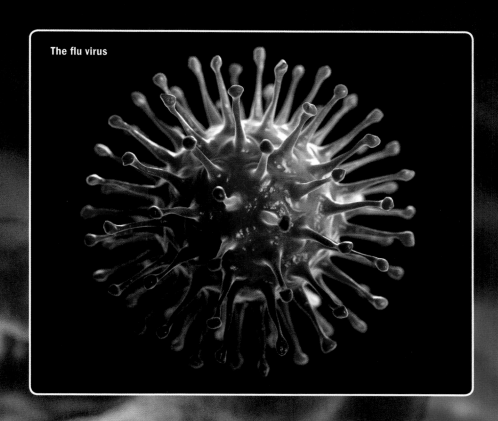

The flu virus

2 **Learn new words.** Listen and repeat. TR: 16

3 **Work in pairs.** What do you do to protect yourself against disease? Give two or three examples.

4 Read and circle the correct word.

Pardis Sabeti is a doctor and a researcher. In her recent research on the *antibiotic / virus* that causes Lassa Fever, she wanted to find out why some people get the *disease / cell* and others don't. Pardis didn't just do research in her lab. She traveled to hospitals in Africa to learn more about diseases. There, she helped train medical workers to *treat / digest* people. She hopes that one day her research will help scientists to make a *symptom / vaccination* available that can *protect / invade* people against Lassa Fever.

5 Learn new words. Listen for these words and match them to the definitions. Then listen and repeat.
TR: 17 and 18

emotion	illness	positive	to survive

_____ 1. state of being sick

_____ 2. confident and happy

_____ 3. continue to live

_____ 4. feeling

Scientist Pardis Sabeti is also in a rock band, Thousand Days.

6 Choose an activity. Work in pairs.

1. Make a list of three health problems in your country. Then write the causes of these problems.

2. Pardis is hardworking and creative. Do you have either of these traits? If so, what do you use them for?

3. If you could find the cure for one disease, which disease would it be and why? Discuss. Then share your responses with the class.

Checking in with friends	Saying how you feel
Are you OK?	Yeah, I'm fine. / Not really. I feel <u>awful</u>.
Are you feeling better?	Yeah, I'm starting to. / No, I feel worse. I need <u>to go home</u>.
Is anything wrong?	No, everything's OK. / Actually, I'm feeling pretty <u>sick</u>.

7 **Listen.** How does Myriam check in on her friend? Write the phrases you hear. TR: 20

8 **Read and complete the dialogue.**

Yuto: Hey, Aiko. _____

Aiko: Actually, _____

Yuto: That's too bad! Do you want to go to the nurse?

Aiko: That might be a good idea. _____

Yuto: Come on, I'll walk with you.

(*A little while later . . .*)

Aiko: Hi, Yuto. Thanks for your help earlier.

Yuto: No problem. _____

Aiko: Yeah, _____ I think

that by tomorrow, I'll feel just fine.

9 **Work in pairs.** Play Tic-Tac-Talk. Choose X or O. Then choose a square, and use the words on that square to check in on your friend. Mark your letter (X or O) for a correct sentence. Then your friend chooses a square and responds to your question. Try to get three in a row.

tired	need	better
OK	go home	worse
wrong	feel	sick

Is anything wrong?

Actually, I'm feeling pretty tired.

10 **Work in groups.** Why is it important to talk to friends about how you feel? Do you ever feel like you don't want to tell a friend how you feel physically and emotionally? How could you politely express this?

Adverbs: Saying how and how often you do something

Many teenagers like to sleep **often**. They're **always** tired.

Many people **rarely** get enough sleep. They can get sick more **easily**.

If you sleep **regularly**, you're **usually** able to pay more attention in school.

11 **Read and circle the correct word.**

If you're like a lot of teens, you like to sleep. And that's a good thing! But many people sleep *always / poorly* , and this has harmful effects on the body and mind. While you sleep, your body *well / regularly* produces cells that work to fight infections. If you don't sleep *enough / easily* , fewer cells are produced, and your immune system doesn't work as *effectively / always* . As a result, you can become sick more *rarely / easily* , especially when you don't get enough sleep.

Lack of sleep also affects your mind. You're more likely to feel angry or depressed, so you react *negatively / usually* to almost everything. A lack of sleep makes it difficult to pay attention *rarely / carefully* to what's happening in school. Making good decisions, solving problems, and remembering *always / poorly* seem much harder when you don't get a good night's sleep. Lack of sleep also makes you react to things more *sometimes / slowly* . In fact, tired drivers may be responsible for around twenty percent of all traffic accidents. Sleeping at least seven hours a night is important for your health, your grades, and even your safety!

12 **Work in pairs.** You learned that sleep is important. Talk about the benefits of sleeping well. Use words from the box in your discussion.

| always | calmly | clearly | effectively | often | regularly | usually |

A good night's sleep helps me think clearly.

13 **Learn new words.** Read and listen to information about the connection between sleep and intelligence. Then listen and repeat. **TR: 22 and 23**

Researchers that study sleep and the **brain** have a **theory**: getting enough **rest** is strongly connected with intelligence. Just as humans prefer to sleep in **comfortable** beds, highly intelligent animals like these chimpanzees **select** the strongest trees for a good night's sleep.

14 **Work in pairs.** Talk about your own sleep habits. Do you sleep well? What affects your sleep? Why? Use the words in the box to help you.

comfortable	enough	nervous	poorly
rest	select	stress	well

15 **Work in groups.** Design a bedroom that would result in really good sleep. Draw your design. Explain why the room is good for getting enough sleep. Use adverbs to talk about how the room helps people sleep. Present your information to the class.

16 **Before you read, discuss in pairs.** Based on the title and the image, what do you think this reading is about?

17 **Learn new words.** Find these words in the reading. What do you think they mean? Use a dictionary to check. Pay attention to how each word is used in a sentence in the dictionary. Then listen and repeat. TR: 24

adolescent	experience	process	structure

18 **While you read, summarize each paragraph.** TR: 25

THE
Teenage Brain

Shaping your future

1   Being a teenager can be challenging, but it can also be exciting. You're becoming more independent and making decisions for yourself. You are also learning to take risks and solve problems better than you could before. And changes are happening throughout your body, even in your brain.

2   You can't see the changes in your brain, but they're affecting how you develop into an adult. At this time in your life, there is a process going on inside your brain that makes it work faster and more efficiently. Imagine that the structure of your brain is like a big road map. There are lots of roads leading to different destinations. When you were a child, as you learned new things, your brain created more and more roads leading to different destinations. By the time you become an adolescent, the most important places on the map have many different roads leading to them. Now your brain's job is to make that map more efficient. It removes the roads that you don't need and works to make the other roads faster.

3   As a result, your experiences as a teenager actually affect the way that your brain develops. If you spend hours playing video games, what skills do you use? You learn to see something with your eyes and respond to it with your hands, right? As you develop those skills, your brain is making sure that the roads leading to them are especially fast and efficient. So, your video-game playing could be preparing you for a career such as a fighter pilot, or even a surgeon.

4   This is a great time for you to practice new skills and discover what you're good at and what you love doing. Go out and try different activities, and stick with them if you think they're useful. Remember that with everything you do, you're shaping your brain for the future.

19 After you read, work in pairs to answer the questions.

1. What does the writer compare the structure of the brain to?
2. What happened to your brain as you learned new things as a child?
3. How does the brain become more efficient when you are an adolescent?
4. How can your experiences as a teenager affect the development of your brain?
5. What is the writer's advice for teenagers?

20 Match these summaries to the correct paragraph. Write the number on the line.

_____ What you do as an adolescent affects your brain's development.

_____ Your brain forms many connections when you are a child, and then it makes them more efficient when you are a teenager.

_____ It is important to try to have lots of new experiences when you are a teenager.

_____ Teenagers experience a lot of changes.

21 Discuss in groups.

1. How do some of the activities you enjoy doing now provide you with important skills for the future? Give examples.

2. Knowing that what you do shapes your brain, what activities shouldn't you do? Why shouldn't you do them? Give one or two examples.

3. Name three interesting careers. Then imagine what activities a teenager could do now to shape their brains for each career.

33

VIDEO ▷

22 **Before you watch, discuss in pairs.** How can each of the following affect your emotions?

diet	health	other people
school	sleep	surroundings

23 **Work in pairs.** The title of this video is *The Forgotten Organ*. An *organ* is a part of the body with a special task, such as the heart. What do you think the "forgotten organ" is? Discuss your ideas.

24 Watch scene 2.1. **While you watch, answer the questions.** According to the video, what is the "forgotten organ"? Was your answer from Activity 23 correct?

25 **After you watch, work in pairs to answer the questions.**

1. What are microbes?

2. What part of your body is almost equal in weight to all the microbes in your body?

3. How many bacteria are in your gut?

4. How do the microbes in your gut send signals to your brain?

5. When Elaine Hsiao observed communication between two mice, what did she notice about the mouse with no microbes?

6. What happened when she put microbes back into the mouse?

26 **Work in groups.** Some bacteria and viruses are harmful. Discuss examples of harmful microbes. Describe a time when harmful microbes made you sick. How did you treat the situation?

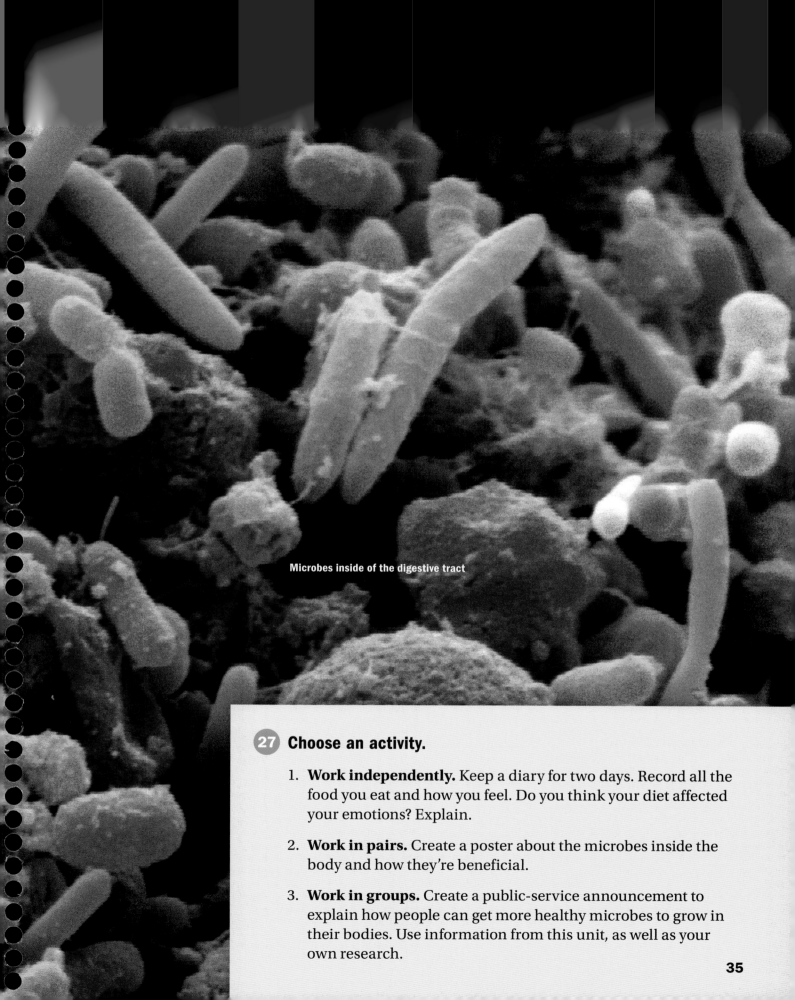

Microbes inside of the digestive tract

27 Choose an activity.

1. **Work independently.** Keep a diary for two days. Record all the food you eat and how you feel. Do you think your diet affected your emotions? Explain.

2. **Work in pairs.** Create a poster about the microbes inside the body and how they're beneficial.

3. **Work in groups.** Create a public-service announcement to explain how people can get more healthy microbes to grow in their bodies. Use information from this unit, as well as your own research.

GRAMMAR TR: 26

Make + adjective: Saying what affects mood and feelings

A lack of sleep **makes** you tired.

Does exercise **make** you feel good?

Some viruses **make** us very sick.

Can this medicine **make** you better?

28 **Read.** Complete the sentences to say how these things make people feel.

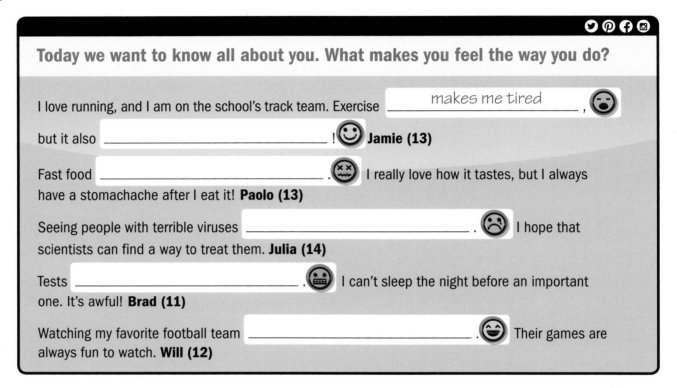

Today we want to know all about you. What makes you feel the way you do?

I love running, and I am on the school's track team. Exercise ___makes me tired___ , 😩 but it also _____ ! ☺ **Jamie (13)**

Fast food _____ . 😵 I really love how it tastes, but I always have a stomachache after I eat it! **Paolo (13)**

Seeing people with terrible viruses _____ . ☹ I hope that scientists can find a way to treat them. **Julia (14)**

Tests _____ . 😬 I can't sleep the night before an important one. It's awful! **Brad (11)**

Watching my favorite football team _____ . 😄 Their games are always fun to watch. **Will (12)**

29 **Work independently.** Use *make* to say how each of the following affects you.

1. A strong immune system ___makes me feel healthy.___ _____

2. A virus can _____

3. Good bacteria can _____

4. A good night's sleep _____

30 **Work in pairs.** Take turns tossing the cube. Say what makes you feel the emotion.

A good video game makes me excited.

Really? Video games make me feel bored. Action movies make me excited.

Go to p. 157.

36

WRITING

When we write a classification essay, we divide the topic into different categories. Then we present each category and support it with examples. The following phrases are useful when classifying:

additionally	another type/way	to begin with	the final type/way

31 **Read the model.** Work in pairs to identify the different categories in the essay. Underline words that signal the categories.

When people hear the word *stress*, they usually think of something negative. However, stress can have several benefits for the body and mind. To begin with, there is the type of stress people feel when there is something important to do. For example, some students are stressed before a big test. The stress might make them feel nervous, but it also makes them feel focused. This type of stress can help people work efficiently to meet their goals.

Another way stress benefits us is by keeping us healthy. Scientists who study stress learned that a little stress strengthens the immune system. When your body learns to respond to some stress, it's able to protect you from infection better.

The final way that stress benefits us is by helping us react to danger. If you see a car coming around the corner too fast, you might experience stress. This stress sends a message to warn your brain of danger, allowing your body to respond quickly. Without the stress, you may not be able to jump out of the car's way soon enough.

Of course, too much stress is harmful to our bodies and minds. But the right amount of stress makes us more efficient, healthier, and safer.

32 **Work in pairs.** What are the three benefits of stress mentioned in the essay?

33 **Write.** Write a classification essay about the negative effects of stress. Give examples.

NATIONAL GEOGRAPHIC

Take Care of Yourself

"Taking care of others can only happen if you first take care of yourself."

—Pardis Sabeti

National Geographic Explorer, Computational Geneticist

1. **Watch scene 2.2.**

2. Pardis says that you first have to take care of yourself before you can help others. Do you agree with her? Why or why not? Do you take care of yourself? What could you do to improve?

3. How do you balance work and fun in your life? What are your daily responsibilities? What do you do for fun? Do you have enough time for both? Explain.

Make an Impact

A **Create a brochure about healthy living.**

- Find out about the importance of sleep, vaccinations, exercise, and healthy food.

- Organize your findings in a brochure. Include photos and drawings.

- Present your brochure to the class.

B **Plan and conduct sleep research.**

- Write five questions to find out how well your classmates sleep.

- Survey at least ten classmates. Summarize the results.

- Present the information to the class.

C **Plan and hold a microbial quiz show.**

- Prepare cards with different facts about viruses and bacteria.

- Organize two teams in your class.

- Hold the quiz show. Read each fact aloud. Classmates say if you're describing a virus or bacteria.

Express Yourself

1 **Read and listen to the song *One Truth* by Pardis Sabeti's band, Thousand Days.** TR: 27

ONE TRUTH

I'm sitting in here in this room
Watching everything move
I do not know how this city was built
We are forsaken to the sound
Oh that life that goes
But we were born to radiate

We are gathered on the ground
Waiting for a sign to arrive
Looking for the answers in the
    starry sky
But we were home all along
    and we are the light
We think, we speak, we walk, we
    breathe the air

Yeah
A lifetime that we write
We laugh
We cry
We pray
We are love
We dream
We scream
We strive
Our hunger will never die
I'm here in this fight, always

A lifetime for one for one truth
That I'm alive, And so are you
We are here, We are the proof
Yeah

A lifetime for one
For one truth

2 Discuss in groups.

1. Pardis recorded this song with other scientists while fighting the Ebola virus. They saw many people, including friends, die of the virus. This made them very sad. To help, they recorded this song. What is the "one truth" that they are singing about?

2. Do you like the song? Why or why not?

3 Connect ideas. In Unit 1, you learned about colors. In Unit 2, you learned about health. What is the connection between these two units? How can colors affect your body and your mind?

4 Choose an activity.

1. Choose a topic:
   - how colors make you feel
   - body and mind

2. Choose a way to express yourself:
   - a song
   - a poem
   - a piece of graphic art

3. Present your work.

Your Virtual Self

"Really good technology helps us all be more human and connect with each other as we never could before."

—Amber Case

This girl is wearing a high-tech armband that can find her friends nearby, send text messages, and even act as a video-game controller.

1. Look at the photo. Have you ever used anything similar to this type of technology? Explain.

2. What technology do you use in your daily life? Think about your home, your schoolwork, and your free-time activities.

3. Imagine you don't have a cell phone. How would you contact your friends? Explain.

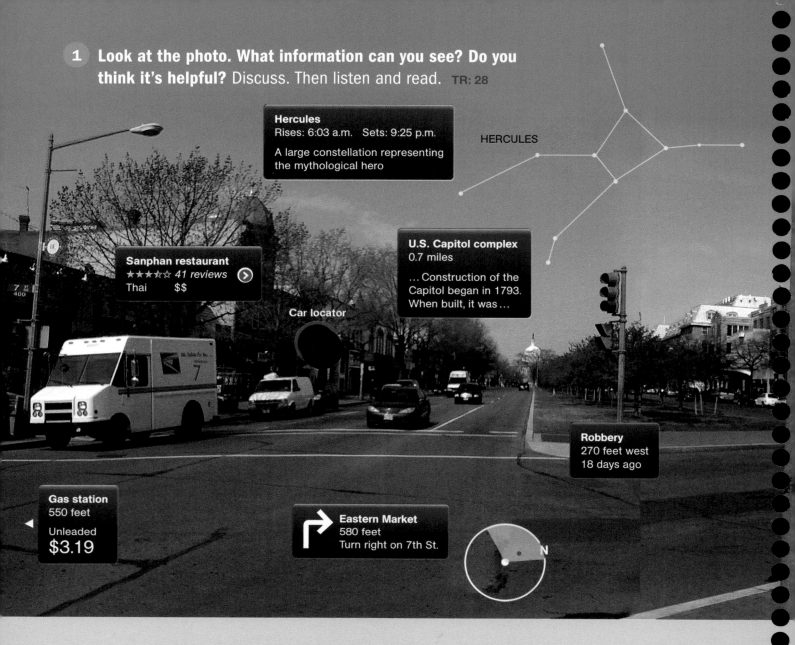

Hercules
Rises: 6:03 a.m.   Sets: 9:25 p.m.
A large constellation representing the mythological hero

HERCULES

Sanphan restaurant
★★★☆☆ 41 reviews
Thai $$

Car locator

U.S. Capitol complex
0.7 miles
… Construction of the Capitol began in 1793. When built, it was …

Robbery
270 feet west
18 days ago

Gas station
550 feet
Unleaded
$3.19

Eastern Market
580 feet
Turn right on 7th St.

N

Anthropologists traditionally study human behavior and culture. They look at the way humans live and work together. Amber Case is an anthropologist, but she studies a different type of anthropology. Amber is a cyborg anthropologist. Do you know what a cyborg is? Part human, part **machine**, a cyborg is usually associated with science fiction movies or comic books.

Amber believes that in today's **digital** world, we're all cyborgs. We rely on **technology** all the time. Our cell phones and tablet computers are like extra body parts that we carry around with us. "Our cell phones have become like children," explains Amber. "If they cry, we pick them up. We plug them into the wall and feed them. When they're lost, we panic."

In the past, we humans developed **tools** that extended our physical **abilities**. We used them to **improve** the environment, farm the land, move around faster, or protect ourselves. In the twenty-first century, our smart tools— our gadgets—extend our mental abilities. With

622-624 North Carolina Ave. SE
900 feet

List price: **$2,995,000**
Bed: **7**   Bath: **8**
On market: **420 days**

flickr: Eastern Market Fire
510 feet

Taken: 2007-04-30
09:35:35 a.m.

Peregrine Espresso
195 feet

Free Wi-Fi

Bus stop
70 feet

Nearest for

32 34 36
A11 C40
CIRC

Subway stop
140 feet

Nearest for
● Orange Line
● Blue Line

Twitter users in the area

perfect day to head to @EasternMarketDC
anyone want to meet up? #spring #dc #market
Posted by @ARpro 10 minutes ago

modern technology, we can **communicate** faster and find any **information** we want in an **instant**. **Social media** allows us to connect with people around the world. So friendships can form based on our shared interests, not just our **location**.

Although there are a lot of positive things about technology, Amber thinks there is also a negative side to our new cyborg selves. She worries that our **constant access** to other people interferes with our ability to just be alone. Wherever we are, there's someone we know who's online and ready to interact with us. "We aren't taking time to slow down and figure out who we really are," says Amber.

Despite these concerns, Amber doesn't think that machines are taking over. "We're sharing with each other—human to human—in a very real way."

2 **Learn new words.** Listen and repeat.
TR: 29

3 **Work in pairs.** Do you agree that you're a cyborg? Why or why not?

45

4 Read and write the words from the list.

access	communicate	constant	digital
information	location	social media	technology

According to Amber Case, in today's world of _____ , people have two selves. There's the real self, and then there is a second self—the _____ self. This is the person that you become when you go online. There are some risks to having a virtual identity. Through your virtual self, you create huge amounts of _____ about yourself that anyone can _____ . Another problem is that you're never really alone. People still _____ with your virtual self when you're not there. Even when you're sleeping, your friends are using their smartphones to connect with you on _____ . This _____ online interaction means it's very difficult to disconnect!

5 Learn new words. Listen for these words and match them to the definitions. Then listen and repeat. TR: 30 and 31

to extend	to interfere	to rely on	to take over

_____ 1. take control of

_____ 2. make something larger

_____ 3. feel that you can't be without

_____ 4. get in the way of something

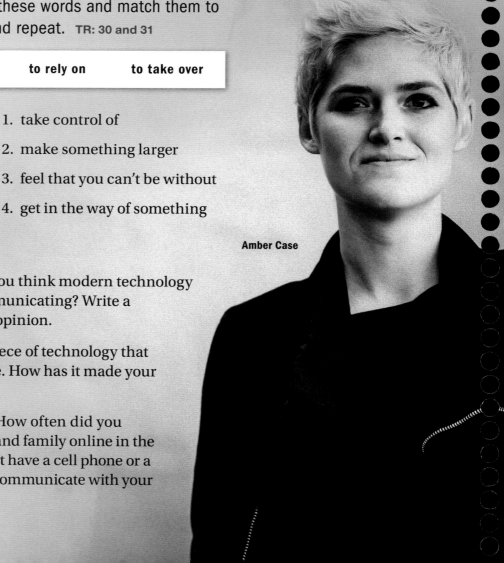

Amber Case

6 Choose an activity.

1. **Work independently.** Do you think modern technology has made us better at communicating? Write a paragraph to explain your opinion.

2. **Work in pairs.** Discuss a piece of technology that has really changed your life. How has it made your life easier?

3. **Work in groups.** Discuss. How often did you communicate with friends and family online in the last week? Imagine you don't have a cell phone or a computer. How would you communicate with your friends and family?

7 **Listen.** How do the speakers check that they understand each other? Write the phrases you hear. TR: 33

8 **Read and complete the dialogue.**

Carla: Twenty years from now, I doubt that anyone will have a cell phone.

Santana: Seriously? Do _____ that we won't talk on the phone in the future?

Carla: No, _____ . I just think that we'll have technology in our brains. So then we won't need to carry anything with us.

Santana: _____ that we'll all have tiny machines in our heads?

Carla: _____

Santana: No way! I don't agree. I think we'll have more wearable technology.

Carla: Wearable technology? _____ mean things like special glasses or watches?

Santana: Yes. That's _____ . These gadgets are already out there. But in the future, they'll be much cheaper so that anybody can buy them.

Carla: Maybe you're right. And I like that better than the idea of a machine in my head!

9 **Work in pairs.** Spin the wheel to make a prediction about the topic you land on. Your partner will check for understanding.

People won't drive in the future.

Do you mean that cars won't need drivers?

That's right.

10 **Discuss in groups.** Why is it important to check that you understand something? What might happen if you get the wrong idea about what someone is saying?

Go to p. 157.

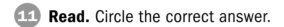

11 **Read.** Circle the correct answer.

The Internet is great, and it gives you the ability to do a lot of things. You *can / should* learn about some really interesting topics and find people who have the same interests as you. But at the same time, you *must / shouldn't* always think about what you say and do online. You *don't have to / should* remember that real people with real feelings are reading your words. You *should / can't* behave the same way online as you behave in real life. Everyone says mean things sometimes, but when you write something online, it will always be there for everyone to see. You *may / have to* say things you don't believe, but you *can / can't* ignore other people's feelings. When you talk to people in real life, they can see your face and your body language. Online, they just read your words so you *can't / have to* be very careful about the words you choose.

12 **Work in pairs.** Write advice using *can, may, should, must,* and *have to.*

1. Someone is mean to you online.

   _____

2. A stranger sends you a message on social media.

   _____

3. You want to start your own blog.

   _____

4. Someone uses a photo of you without asking you first.

   _____

13 **Work in groups.** Take turns discussing problems at school or online. Give advice using *can, may, should, must,* or *have to.*

> I forgot my password for the school website.

> You should send an e-mail to the computer teacher.

48

14 **Learn new words.** Listen to learn about online safety. Then listen and repeat. TR: 35 and 36

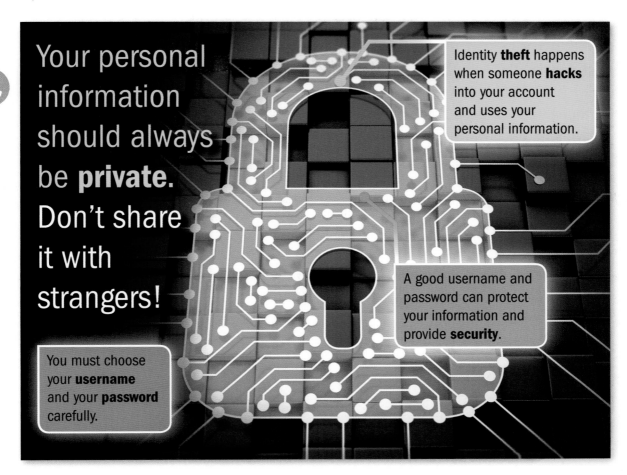

Your personal information should always be **private.** Don't share it with strangers!

Identity **theft** happens when someone **hacks** into your account and uses your personal information.

A good username and password can protect your information and provide **security**.

You must choose your **username** and your **password** carefully.

15 **Work in pairs.** Imagine that you want to start a new social media website. How can you make sure that it's safe? Make a list of five guidelines for users to follow. Use the words in the box, as well as *can, may, should, must,* and *have to.*

hack	information	password	private	theft	username

1. _____

2. _____

3. _____

4. _____

5. _____

16 **Discuss in groups.** People hack into businesses, banks, government websites, and personal e-mail accounts. What information do they want to find? What can they do with this information? What should you do if your own account gets hacked?

17 **Before you read, discuss in pairs.** Based on the title, the photo, and the graphics, what do you think the reading is about?

18 **Learn new words.** Find these words in the reading. What do you think they mean? Use a thesaurus to find synonyms for each word. Then listen and repeat. TR: 37

to demand	edge
to focus	to interrupt

19 **While you read, think about your own home and the technology you use there.** TR: 38

20 **After you read, look at the sentences.** Check T for *true* or F for *false*.

1. Amber Case invented the idea of calm technology. T F

2. Calm technology demands our attention at all times. T F

3. A smoke alarm is an example of calm technology. T F

4. Cooking your food on the stovetop is an example of calm technology. T F

5. Amber believes that houses in the future will use calm technology. T F

21 **Work in pairs.** List three examples from your life where technology has demanded your attention. Then list three examples of calm technology in your school or home. Share your responses with the class.

Calm Down

Should we be excited about calm technology?

Often it seems like technology is everywhere. Computers and smartphones are at the center of almost everything we do. They're constantly demanding our attention. We text our friends during the day, sleep with our devices by our beds, and check our messages as soon as we wake up.

According to Amber Case, in the future, technology will no longer be interrupting us all of the time. Instead, we will use calm technology—a concept first developed by scientist Mark Weiser in the 1970s. In his vision, calm technology works quietly but constantly, at the edge of our attention. We know it is there, but we don't focus on it. According to Mark, the best technology should be invisible and let you live your life.

We already use many different types of calm technology in our everyday lives. Do you have a smoke alarm in your house? That smoke alarm is always there, checking the air for smoke and quietly keeping you safe. It only reminds you it's there when you've burned your toast! Or there may be lights in your home or school that are sensitive to movement. When somebody passes in front of their sensor, the lights turn on. You don't think about this type of technology until you see the light go on. Even a microwave oven is an example of calm technology. You're not standing at the stovetop heating your food: the microwave is doing it for you. You don't think about its work until you hear the beeping noise signaling that your food is ready.

In the future, Amber imagines that our houses will use calm technology to open the curtains for us in the morning, to turn down the heat when we leave, or even to choose the best music for our mood. The minute we walk in the door, our house will respond by turning on the lights and music, setting the heater to a comfortable temperature, and perhaps even starting to prepare our dinner!

22 Discuss in groups.

1. Amber believes that eventually, with calm technology, electronic devices will do all the boring, repetitive tasks in our lives. How will this benefit us? What negative impact might this have on us?

2. Calm technology will allow different machines in our lives to share information about us, our routines, and our personal habits. Do you think that sharing this information is a security risk? Why or why not?

3. Design a house that uses calm technology. Think of all the ways it can use calm technology to make our lives easier without demanding our attention.

VIDEO▷

23 **Before you watch, discuss in pairs.**

1. When you're communicating with your friends, does speed matter? Do you expect your friends to respond instantly? Why or why not?

2. When might you want to slow communication down? Why?

24 **Work in pairs.** You are going to watch a video called *The Distance Between Two Points*. Before you watch, do the following:

1. Draw two points on a sheet of paper. Label them *A* and *B*.

   A
   •

            B
            •

2. Now draw the shortest route from point *A* to point *B*.

3. How could you make this route even shorter?

25 Watch scene 3.1. **While you watch, check your responses.** How does Amber say the distance between two points is made shorter? Does your response from Activity 24 match what she says?

Singers joining in a virtual choir

26 **After you watch, read the sentences.** Circle the correct answer.

1. Amber's dad said that a straight line *was* / *wasn't* always the shortest distance between two points.

2. Amber thinks technology *reduces* / *creates* the distance between two people.

3. Amber studies how technology *affects culture* / *must be used all the time*.

4. With *calm technology* / *social media* , others can interact with our virtual selves when we're not there.

5. Amber created an interface that tells her phone when *she's home* / *her family members are online*.

6. Amber believes that people *sometimes need distance from* / *need constant access to* one another.

27 **Work in pairs.** What technology might you use in each of the places below? When might it be a problem to use technology at each place?

gym	home	library
museum	school	

28 **Choose an activity.**

1. **Work independently.** Imagine you can send a letter back in time to your great-great grandparents. Write a description of a smartphone.

2. **Work in pairs.** Amber's phone has an invisible interface so that it knows when she's home. How could your phone help you based on your location? What kinds of things could it do? Give at least three ideas.

3. **Work in groups.** Think about how communication has changed over the past 100 years. Create a timeline showing at least five ways that communication has changed. Then add two or three predictions for how communication will change in the future.

29 **Read.** The information below came from the Internet. Some sentences are true and some are false. Use *must*, *might*, and *can't* to write what you believe.

1. Giant tortoises can live for one year without food or water. That must be true! My own pet turtle can live without food for a while. / That can't be true! All animals need to eat and drink.

2. There were computers during World War II. _____

3. You only use 10 percent of your brain. _____

4. On average, kids spend over 150 hours a week using technology.
_____
_____

5. There are robots that can play soccer.
_____
_____

6. More people die every year from vending machine accidents than from shark attacks. _____
_____

30 **Work in groups.** Write two true sentences and one false sentence on a piece of paper. Read your sentences to the group. Can they guess the false sentence?

Number 2 must be false. Your house can't be 100 years old—it's too modern!

1. My mom knows how to fly a helicopter.
2. My house is 100 years old.
3. I have fifteen cousins.

WRITING

In an opinion essay, we want to tell others what we believe about a topic. We use facts to support our argument. We must make it clear when we're stating a fact and when we're expressing an opinion.

Facts include:
· a date or time of an event
· a statistic
· a description of an event

Opinions include what the author:
· believes is possible
· thinks about something
· says is good, bad, important, etc.

31 **Read the model.** Work in pairs. Circle the sentences stating facts. Underline the sentences expressing opinions.

An early personal computer

Can we live without computers?

For most people my age, it's hard to imagine life without a computer. It seems like almost everybody has one! In fact, there are 640 million personal computers in households around the world. Most people use them every day for work and play. Actually, the first personal computer was invented in 1975. Before then, people survived without computers and the Internet, so it must be possible!

I believe that there would be some advantages to life without a computer. We would probably do more exercise because we wouldn't be sitting in front of our screens all day. Maybe we would get better at remembering things because we couldn't always check facts online. I think we would also interact more with each other because computers wouldn't demand so much of our attention.

However, I think that it would also be very difficult for young people today to live without computers. We use them to communicate with our friends and family all around the world. We also use computers to research information about many different subjects. Computer technology has helped improve our lives in many different areas. For example, mechanics use computers to check our cars, doctors use computers to analyze health tests, and architects use computers to design modern, safe buildings.

In conclusion, although I think that we may have had healthier lifestyles in our computer-free past, I believe that, in today's society, we can't live without computers.

32 **Work in pairs.** Do you agree with the writer's opinion? Think of one more argument against and one more argument in favor of life without computers. Use facts to support your arguments.

33 **Write.** Write an opinion essay to answer the question: Can we live without smartphones?

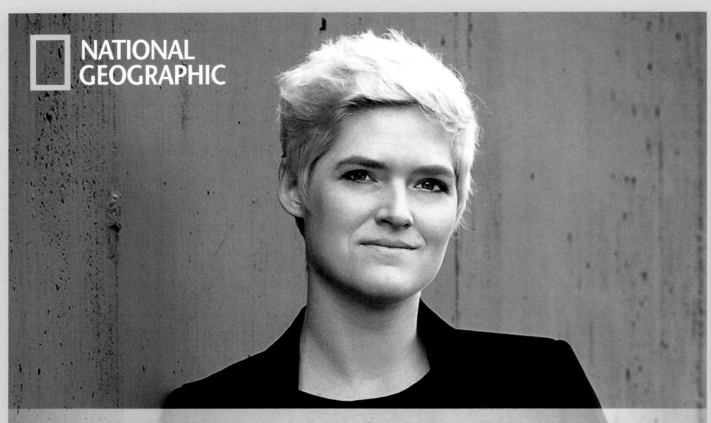

NATIONAL GEOGRAPHIC

Connect with People

"Today's technology extends our mental self. It's changing the way we experience the world."

—Amber Case

National Geographic Explorer, Cyborg Anthropologist

1. Watch scene 3.2.

2. What are your favorite ways to connect with people now? Is it the same for everybody in your life? Explain.

3. How will technology change our communication in the future? Will it help or harm communication? Explain.

Make an Impact

A **Plan and conduct a survey.**

· Write questions to find out about your classmates' online activity.

· Conduct the survey and summarize the results.

· Present the results and make recommendations.

B **Advertise an app or website.**

· Choose an app or a website that you use regularly.

· Write a list of its best and worst features.

· Create an ad for the app or website. Present it to the class.

C **Plan and hold a technology fair.**

· In a group, bring in five or six different technological gadgets.

· Write a short description of each piece. Display your descriptions with the gadgets.

· Hold a technology fair. Discuss how each item is used with your classmates.

Underwater Mysteries

"What's really exciting is having the opportunity to explore anywhere in the world, and share discoveries with everyone in the world."

—Katy Croff Bell

Exploring a shipwreck near Key Largo, Florida, USA

1. Look at the photo and then read the caption. Does it surprise you? Why or why not? Would you like to explore something like this? Explain.

2. Why do people explore underwater? Think of as many different reasons as possible.

3. Imagine you can explore anywhere in the world. Where will you go? Why?

1 **How can technology make underwater exploration easier?** Discuss. Then listen and read. TR: 40

Exploring underwater used to be very difficult. Every **expedition** would take careful preparation, and underwater explorers had no way to communicate with people on land. In fact, we landed on the moon before we started to explore our biggest underwater mountain range, the Mid-Oceanic Ridge. But thanks to technology, all of that is changing. Now, we can explore the deep sea without ever leaving home!

Katy Croff Bell is a leader on E/V *Nautilus*—a ship that explores the oceans. One week the **destination** might be the Gulf of Mexico, in an **attempt** to find a shipwreck.

The next week, *Nautilus* will be on a **journey** to investigate underwater volcanoes near Grenada. Scientists on the ship send robotic **vehicles** deep into the sea to **look for** shipwrecks, to study the plants and animals, and to look at the geology, or rocks, in an area. The vehicles transmit images and information back to the scientists on the ship. It's a great way to explore deep and dangerous places. And robots aren't the only cool technology on *Nautilus*.

Let's say you want to find out where *Nautilus* is right now. Well, you can go **online** to see. The *Nautilus* **website** has a 24-hour

E/V *Nautilus* uses robotic vehicles like this one to explore deep waters.

webcam so that people all around the world can find out what's happening on the ship at any time of day or night. Telepresence technology allows you to be a **virtual** explorer on *Nautilus*. You can also **follow** the updates on the *Nautilus* **blog** and send **messages** to scientists on the ship. Some people even get the **opportunity** to help out with the research! Scientists can communicate with **experts** on the other side of the world and make sure that they have **accurate** information about their discoveries. For example, when researchers on *Nautilus* discovered an aircraft on the ocean floor near Sicily, World War II pilots helped them identify it. "The telepresence system allows people from schoolchildren to research scientists to be a part of our expeditions," says Katy. "It's really exciting!"

2 **Learn new words.** Listen and repeat. TR: 41

3 **Work in pairs.** Imagine you're communicating with the scientists on E/V *Nautilus*. What questions do you want to ask? What do you think the ship might discover during your virtual visit?

4 **Read and write the words from the list.** Make any necessary changes.

attempt	blog	destination	expert
journey	message	online	opportunity

In 2013, *Nautilus* was on a _____ through the Caribbean Sea. Its _____ was the Kick'Em Jenny volcano, near the island of Grenada. The scientists were making an _____ to learn more about the volcano's last big eruption. But when they started to dive around the volcano, they discovered that chemicals from the volcano created a perfect environment for a lot of different organisms. It was a wonderful _____ for the scientists to study many underwater animals. _____ from all over the world read the *Nautilus* _____ and saw the video footage _____ . Then they sent _____ to *Nautilus*, asking for samples of all the different organisms. "It was probably the most exciting dive of the season!" says Katy.

5 **Learn new words.** Listen for these words and match them to the definitions. Then listen and repeat. TR: 42 and 43

to find out	to make sure	preparation	to transmit

_____ 1. the act of getting ready

_____ 2. send a signal

_____ 3. learn something

_____ 4. check or confirm something

Katy Croff Bell on E/V *Nautilus*

6 **Choose an activity.**

1. **Work independently.** What do you think a day in the life of a scientist on E/V *Nautilus* is like? What kinds of things do they do? Write a paragraph about a crew member's typical day.

2. **Work in pairs.** Deep-sea exploration is dangerous, difficult, and expensive. With this in mind, make a list of five reasons why we should explore the deep sea.

3. **Work in groups.** Imagine you're a scientist on *Nautilus*. You have made an exciting discovery on the ocean floor. What did you find? How did you find out more about it? How did you tell others? Share with the class.

SPEAKING STRATEGY TR: 44

Making suggestions	Responding to suggestions
How about going scuba diving?	Yes, good idea! / I love that idea, but it isn't a good time of year for that.
It would be great to follow *Nautilus* online for our next project.	Sure. That's a really great suggestion. / Unfortunately, my Internet connection isn't working right now.
We could research underwater volcanoes for the science fair.	OK. Let's do that. / Yes, but we already did volcanoes for last year's presentation.

7 **Listen.** How do the speakers make and respond to suggestions? Write the phrases you hear. **TR: 45**

8 **Read and complete the dialogue.**

Ameira: Do we have any plans for tonight yet?

Nora: Not yet. _____ have a picnic on the beach.

Ameira: _____ , the weather forecast says it's going to rain tonight. It'll be too wet for a picnic. Any other ideas?

Nora: _____ go to the movies. There's a great documentary about underwater exploration that I'd really like to see.

Ameira: _____ I don't really like documentaries.

Nora: OK, well _____ just staying home and checking out the *Nautilus* live feed? The ship's in the Atlantic Ocean, and the crew is looking for shipwrecks near Portugal.

Ameira: Sure! That's a _____

9 **Work in pairs.** Toss the cube and make a suggestion for where to go on a vacation. Your partner will respond to your suggestion. Then switch roles.

> How about exploring an underwater shipwreck?

> I love that idea, but wouldn't that cost a lot of money?

an underwater shipwreck

a cave

a beautiful, sandy beach

Go to p. 159.

10 **Work in groups.** Imagine that visitors from another country are coming to your school, and your class must show them around town. Make and respond to at least four suggestions about what to do with them.

Used to and *would*: **Talking about habits in the past**

Did you use to read about the ocean as a kid?

No, I **never used to be** interested in the ocean, and I **didn't use to read** much at all!

That changed when my dad, who **used to be** a diver, took me diving for the first time, and I saw an old shipwreck.

After that, I **used to / would read** anything about the ocean I could get my hands on!

11 **Read.** Complete the sentences with *used to* or *would* and the verb in parentheses.

In the past, when scientists wanted to do research in the seas, they

_____ (go) out on a ship to collect their information.

Typically, the expeditions _____ (be) several weeks long.

After the expedition, scientists _____ (bring) their data

home with them. They _____ (work) on that information

for several months, and finally they _____ (write) about

their results in a scientific paper. Most people never read this information because it

_____ (be) available only in scientific magazines or newspapers.

A nineteenth-century diving suit

12 **Work in pairs.** Use the information to rewrite sentences about ocean exploration in the early nineteenth century. Use *used to* and *would*.

1. Scientists traveled underwater in submarines or diving bells.
   Scientists would travel underwater in submarines or diving bells.

2. Ships used wind power to travel.

   _____

3. Divers pulled on a lifeline to communicate with people above the water.

   _____

4. Divers were able to breathe with air pumped from the surface.

   _____

13 **Work in pairs.** Tell about your habits in the past.

did you use to	I didn't use to	I never used to	I would always/never	I used to

64

14 **Learn new words.** Listen to learn about the SS *Republic* and her final journey. Then listen and repeat. **TR: 47 and 48**

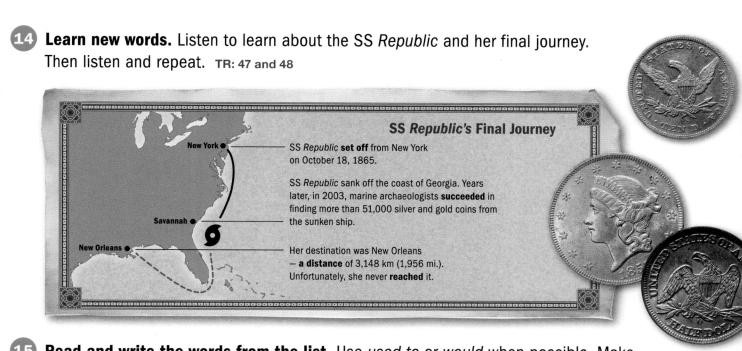

SS *Republic's* Final Journey

SS *Republic* **set off** from New York on October 18, 1865.

SS *Republic* sank off the coast of Georgia. Years later, in 2003, marine archaeologists **succeeded** in finding more than 51,000 silver and gold coins from the sunken ship.

Her destination was New Orleans – **a distance** of 3,148 km (1,956 mi.). Unfortunately, she never **reached** it.

15 **Read and write the words from the list.** Use *used to* or *would* when possible. Make any other necessary changes.

be	distance	reach	set off	succeed	travel

   In the nineteenth century, people _____ by ship more often because there were no airplanes. One ship, SS *Republic*, _____ from New York in 1865. Its destination was New Orleans. New Orleans was a great _____ from New York, and traveling by boat was never completely safe. Journeys such as this _____ difficult and sometimes dangerous because of the weather conditions. Most of the time, the ships _____ in arriving at their destination. However, this was not the case for SS *Republic*, which never _____ New Orleans. The ship sank near the coast of Savannah and wasn't found until 2003.

16 **Work in groups.** Talk about how life used to be for the people traveling on SS *Republic*. Discuss the topics below. Use *used to* and *would*.

- what they did in their free time
- why they carried gold coins
- what they ate
- how they traveled

17 **Before you read, discuss in pairs.** Based on the title and the photo, what do you think the reading is about?

18 **Learn new words.** Find these words in the reading. What do you think they mean? Think about the context of this unit and how the words connect to it. Then listen and repeat. TR: 49

| angle | carving | to examine | to identify | remains |

19 **While you read, think about the author's purpose in writing this text.** TR: 50

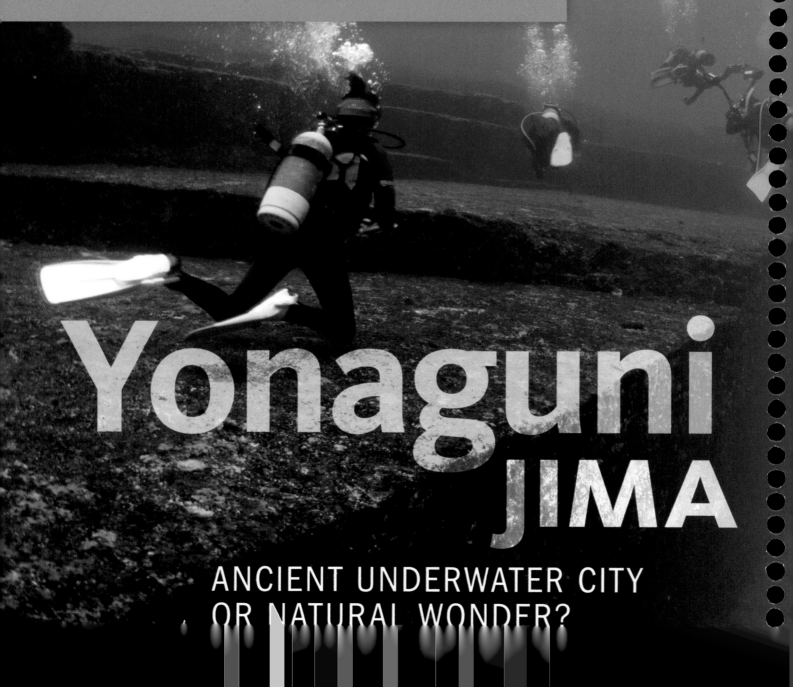

Yonaguni
JIMA
ANCIENT UNDERWATER CITY OR NATURAL WONDER?

Some believe it's an ancient city that sank thousands of years ago. Others think it is a natural structure—the result of many earthquakes in the area. Either way, the huge rock formations and stone structures off the coast of Yonaguni Island are an amazing sight.

The small Japanese island of Yonaguni is 1,029 km (640 mi.) south of the coast of mainland Japan, between the East China Sea and the Pacific Ocean. From November to July, many divers visit Yonaguni to see the hammerhead sharks. In 1986, a local diver, Kihachiro Aratake, was looking for sharks about 18 m (60 ft.) underwater when he discovered an enormous rock shaped like a rectangle. It was about the size of two football fields. There were huge steps on the rock, perfect right angles, and long, straight passages. Was this really just a rock? Or was it something more?

Masaaki Kimura, a marine geologist, traveled to the island to examine the discovery. At first he thought the formations were natural. But then he noticed shapes and carvings on the rock. Masaaki now believes that these rock formations are the remains of an important city more than 5,000 years old. He thinks that it sank in a huge tsunami about 2,000 years ago. Masaaki has identified the ruins of a castle, several temples, and a large stadium in the rock formations.

Some scientists disagree with Kimura. Robert Schoch, also a geologist, thinks that earthquakes caused these rock formations and the "carvings" are just natural scratches on the rock. "I do not believe it is a human-made structure," says Robert. "It is absolutely incredible, and well worth seeing, but it is a natural structure."

Perhaps we will never know the truth about Yonaguni. But one thing is for sure: it's an amazing place to explore.

20 **After you read, work in pairs to answer these questions.**

1. Why do people like to go diving at Yonaguni?

2. Who discovered the rock formations at Yonaguni? How?

3. What did Masaaki Kimura originally think about the rock formations?

4. What does he believe now?

5. According to Robert Schoch, what caused the rock formations?

6. What is the writer's conclusion about Yonaguni?

21 **Work in pairs.** Why did the author write this text? Check the best reason. Then explain your choice.

☐ to express his/her opinion about the rock formations at Yonaguni

☐ to persuade tourists to go diving at Yonaguni

☐ to explain different theories about the rock formations at Yonaguni

☐ to describe the history of Yonaguni

22 **Discuss in groups.**

1. Look closely at the photo. Which theory do you agree with? Why?

2. Do you know of any other underwater discoveries? Are they natural or human-made? What do you know about them?

3. Oceanographer Robert Ballard said, "There's probably more history now preserved underwater than in all the museums of the world combined." Do you agree? Why? What can we learn from artifacts found underwater?

VIDEO ▶

23 **Before you watch, discuss in pairs.** Look at the names of famous creatures. Discuss what you know about each one. Can you think of any others? Why do you think people find them so interesting?

| Bigfoot | El Chupacabra | Dracula | Yeti |

24 **Work in pairs.** You are going to watch a video called *Loch Ness Monster: Mystery Solved?* What do you already know about the Loch Ness Monster? Compare it with the creatures mentioned in Activity 23.

25 Watch scene 4.1. **While you watch, list three words that describe the images of Nessie.**

26 **After you watch, work in pairs to answer the questions.**

1. When was the first sighting of the Loch Ness Monster?

2. Who was Marmaduke Wetherell?

3. When did a photographer take a picture of the Loch Ness Monster underwater?

4. What did Wetherell's stepson confess?

5. What are the two theories about a recent satellite photo?

6. Why do some tourists still visit Loch Ness?

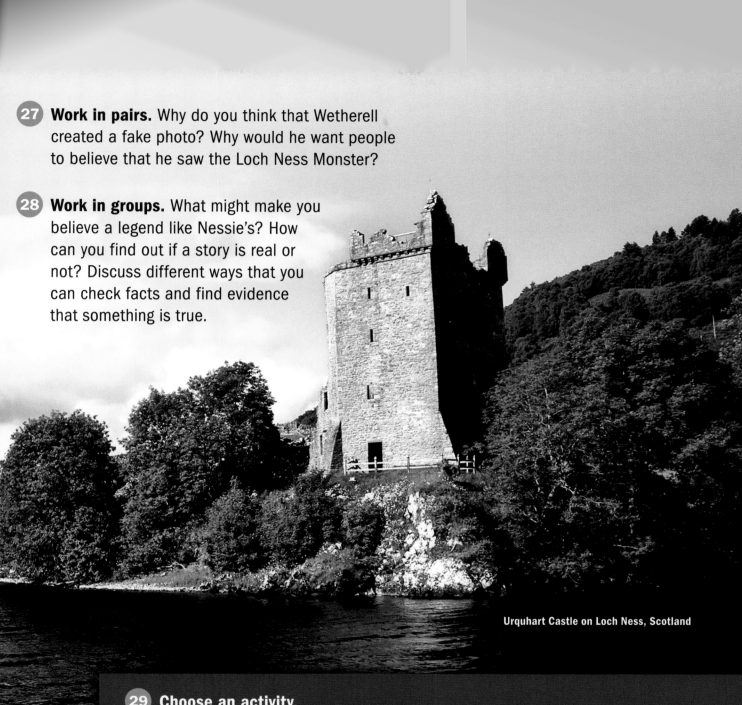

27 **Work in pairs.** Why do you think that Wetherell created a fake photo? Why would he want people to believe that he saw the Loch Ness Monster?

28 **Work in groups.** What might make you believe a legend like Nessie's? How can you find out if a story is real or not? Discuss different ways that you can check facts and find evidence that something is true.

Urquhart Castle on Loch Ness, Scotland

29 **Choose an activity.**

1. **Work independently.** Imagine you visited Loch Ness and spotted Nessie. Write a paragraph about your experience. Describe what you saw, how you felt, and what you did.

2. **Work in pairs.** Create your own legendary monster. Think about where it lives, what it does, what it looks like, and who has seen it. Then write a short newspaper article about a sighting of this monster.

3. **Work in groups.** Prepare a short presentation about the Loch Ness Monster. Use some of the information from this video and some from your own research. Include your own ideas about the truth behind the legend.

Simple past: Describing past actions

When **did** the village **sink**? It **sank thousands of years ago**.

Last October, divers **discovered** a shipwreck in the Indian Ocean.

In 1912, RMS *Titanic* **set off** from Southampton, UK. The ship **didn't arrive** at its destination.

Nautilus **reached** the Gulf of Mexico **the day before yesterday**.

GREAT UNDERWATER DISCOVERIES

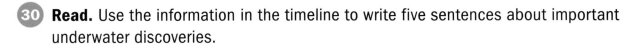

1857
James Alden discovers the Monterey Canyon, an underwater valley in California.

1934
William Beebe makes the first underwater exploration of the ocean in a bathysphere.

1943
Jacques Cousteau and Émile Gagnan invent the Aqua-Lung. It lets divers breathe underwater.

1960
The *Trieste* travels to the Mariana Trench, the deepest part of the world's oceans.

1985
Robert Ballard finds the wreck of the RMS *Titanic*.

2012
Film director and explorer James Cameron becomes the first person to travel alone to the bottom of the Mariana Trench.

30 **Read.** Use the information in the timeline to write five sentences about important underwater discoveries.

More than thirty years ago, Robert Ballard found the wreck of the Titanic.

_____

_____

_____

_____

31 **Work in groups.** Use the photos to tell a story. Say when the action in each photo happened in the past.

> A ship set off on a journey 150 years ago.

> Because of a terrible storm, the ship never arrived at its destination.

When we provide information on a topic, we may talk about more than one idea relating to that topic. When those ideas are different, we can use the following words to show contrast:

although   **but**   **even though**   **however**   **instead**

32 **Read the model.** Work in pairs to identify how the writer contrasts different points of view. Underline the words.

In 1922, a man named Martin Sheffield said he saw a strange creature in Nahuel Huapi Lake in Patagonia, Argentina. It had a long neck and the body of a crocodile. Since then, many other people have said that they've seen the same creature. The local people call it *Nahuelito*. But what's really there?

Some people believe that it could be a plesiosaur—a marine dinosaur. Around 30,000 years ago, the lake was part of the Pacific Ocean. It's possible that, as the climate got warmer and the lake formed, the creature stayed there. However, dinosaur experts think this is impossible because dinosaurs were extinct thousands of years before the lake formed. Other people think that the creature is actually a secret submarine. Although this is an interesting idea, it doesn't explain how the submarine got into the lake and why it has been there for nearly one hundred years. A third theory is that Nahuelito formed because of pollution in the water. But the Nahuel Huapi Lake is not very polluted, so this theory seems unlikely.

Some people don't believe there is anything strange in the lake. Instead, they argue that people are looking at pieces of wood or even sheep swimming in the water. Even though it isn't the most exciting theory, it may be the most sensible!

33 **Work in pairs.** Which of the theories about Nahuelito do you believe? Why?

34 **Write.** Write about a mythical creature from your country. Present contrasting points of view about the creature.

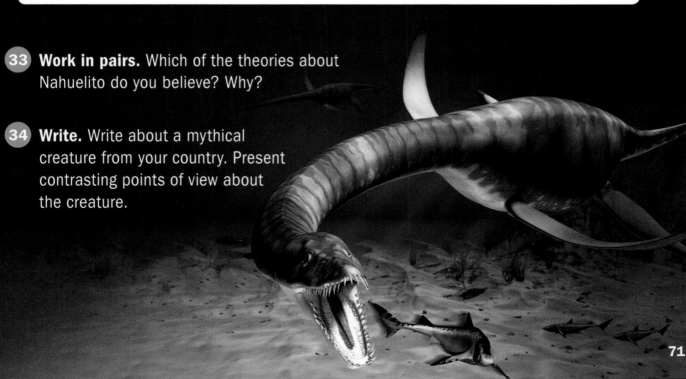

Be Curious

"If you don't have questions about where you're going, then you're not going to be able to answer them or learn new things."

—Katy Croff Bell
National Geographic Explorer, Oceanographer

1. **Watch scene 4.2.**

2. Think about the places you go and the things you use regularly. List three places or things. How much do you know about them? How could you find out more?

3. Choose a place in your region, and make a list of questions that you have about it. Ask about its history, architecture, uses, and the people who go there. Then talk to people in your community to get answers to your questions.

Make an Impact

A **Plan and write a blog entry about underwater exploration.**

· Use the Internet to research popular sites for underwater exploration. Find information about a place you would explore and how you would explore it.

· Imagine you explored this place. Write a blog entry saying how you prepared and what your expedition was like.

· Publish your blog entry. Respond to questions or comments on it.

B **Plan and give a presentation about an underwater city.**

· Find out about an underwater city. Collect photos and drawings.

· Organize your information into a poster or computer-based presentation.

· Make your presentation. Respond to your classmates' questions.

C **Investigate a local body of water.**

· Choose a body of water near your home.

· Find out about the animals and plants that live in this environment.

· Make a model or a poster to show what you learned about the body of water and what lives there.

Express Yourself

1 **Read and listen to Talita's blog entry about her expedition on the E/V *Nautilus*.** TR: 52

The *Nautilus* expedition to the Cayman Islands

Hi! I'm Talita and this is my blog! Enjoy!

Day 1: August 15th

Wow! I can't believe I'm actually here on *Nautilus*! I'm one of five very lucky students taking part in *Nautilus's* four-day expedition to the Cayman Islands. We had a talk from the expedition leader, Dr. Katy Croff Bell, about where we're going and what we'll be doing. Oh, and all the safety stuff as well, of course! I look supercool in my life jacket . . . NOT!

Day 2: August 16th

What an amazing day! In the morning, we met Dr. Robert Ballard, who discovered the wreck of the *Titanic*! After lunch (mahimahi!), we had a tour around *Nautilus*. We looked at the labs, and we went up to the bridge—that's where the captain of the ship works. I even got a chance to steer the ship! (Don't worry, Mom, we're still heading in the right direction . . . I hope!) Later we learned about Hercules—a remotely operated vehicle, or ROV. This robot has so much electronic equipment that I'm amazed it's all waterproof!

Day 3: August 17th

This morning we appeared on the *Nautilus* Live website and talked to middle school students around the world about our expedition. It was awesome—I feel like a real celebrity now! (Except for the clothes . . . and the money . . . OK, maybe not an actual celebrity, but it was pretty cool.) The afternoon was NOT cool, however. There was a big storm, and we all felt very seasick!

My team

Day 4: August 18th

This morning was beautiful, and the sea was calm. Perfect for a dive! Unfortunately, it was Hercules, not us, who got to go diving. What a lucky robot! In the afternoon, we arrived at Grand Cayman. Although I'm sad to leave the *Nautilus* team (especially Hercules), I'm excited to explore the islands and the waters!

ROV Hercules exploring underwater

2 Discuss in pairs.

1. In your opinion, what was the most exciting activity the students did on *Nautilus*?

2. Would you like to take part in an activity like this? Why or why not?

3. Do you read blogs regularly? If so, what kinds of blogs do you like to read? What can you learn from them?

3 Connect ideas.
In Unit 3, you learned about the impact of technology on our lives. In Unit 4, you learned about underwater exploration. How are those topics connected? How can technology help us to learn more about what's underwater?

4 Choose an activity.

1. Choose a topic:
   • connecting with people virtually
   • exploring virtually

2. Choose a way to express yourself:
   • a blog entry
   • a short video journal
   • a poster

3. Present your work.

Life in the Extreme

"When I think about life elsewhere in the universe, it gives me an incredible sense of the fragility of life here on Earth and how important it is to protect our home."
—Kevin Hand

Kevin Hand works in extreme environments.

1. The photo shows Kevin Hand working in Alaska. How do you think he feels in this photo?

2. Name an animal you know that lives in an extremely hot or cold environment. How do you think it's able to survive there?

3. What can we learn about our planet from studying different animals and their habitats?

77

Did you ever wonder how polar bears can **handle** the extreme cold of the Arctic? On a **typical** day, Arctic temperatures can be as low as −30°C (−58°F). That's *really* cold! And what about camels? How can they survive in the heat of the Sahara Desert, where it sometimes reaches 50°C (122°F)? It's because these animals have **adapted** to their **harsh environments**. However, like other **mammals**, the polar bear and the camel can only exist in a certain range of **conditions**. But there are much smaller creatures that can live in far more extreme environments.

One example of an amazing survivor is the tardigrade. Nicknamed the "water bear," this tiny organism is less than a millimeter long. Tardigrades can handle temperatures from −200°C (−328°F) to 151°C (304°F). They can survive despite a **lack of** water and **oxygen**. They can even survive in outer space! In 2011, scientists successfully sent tardigrades to the International Space Station on space shuttle Endeavour.

Apart from the tardigrade, there are many **varieties** of even smaller, single-celled microbes that scientists refer to as *extremophiles*. These microscopic organisms live in some of the harshest environments on the planet. Some live in places where there are very high **levels** of salt, like the Dead Sea. Others live within solid rock. Extremophiles like very hot or very cold environments.

Strain 121, for example, is a type of bacteria with remarkable abilities to tolerate temperatures of 121°C (250°F). It lives on a volcanic vent at the bottom of the Pacific Ocean and feeds on iron! Methanogens, on the other hand, **thrive** under 18 m (60 ft.) of Antarctic ice, where there is no light and no oxygen.

Scientists find these organisms very interesting because they help us understand how **life** might exist on other planets. "We're looking for worlds where [the necessary elements] for life can be found," explains astrobiologist Kevin Hand. "We want to know, what does it take for a world to be habitable?"

A tardigrade or "water bear"

2 **Learn new words.** Listen and repeat. TR: 54

3 **Work in pairs.** Why do scientists study extreme environments and the creatures that live in them?

condition	environment	handle	harsh
lack of	level	thrive	variety

In 2004, National Geographic Explorer Kevin Hand and movie director James Cameron went on a deep-sea expedition to a mid-ocean ridge. There they discovered a _____ of different animals living in this _____ 3,600 m (11,800 ft.) below the surface of the sea. It's a _____ place to live because of the high _____ of poisonous chemicals in the water. There is also a complete _____ light. However, animals like giant tube worms, crabs, and vent fish can _____ these extreme _____ . Although the water is extremely hot and full of chemicals, they don't just survive—they _____ here.

Learn new words. Listen for these words and match them to the synonyms. Then listen and repeat. TR: 55 and 56

creature	to exist	remarkable	to tolerate

1. _____ be

2. _____ animal

3. _____ interesting

4. _____ handle

Choose an activity.

1. **Work independently.** Write a paragraph about how the study of extremophiles could help us to discover life on other planets.

2. **Work in pairs.** Will human activity eventually turn the whole Earth into an extreme environment? Why or why not? Discuss and share your response with the class.

3. **Work in groups.** Conduct a survey to find out what other students think about the possibility of life on other planets. Summarize what you learn for the class.

Giant tubeworms

Expressing strong opinions	Responding
I think <u>the naked mole rat</u> is <u>the ugliest animal</u> around!	Really? I think they're kind of <u>cute</u>.
<u>Slugs</u> are the worst. They're even <u>scarier</u> than <u>snakes</u>.	I don't know. I sort of like <u>slugs</u>.
There's nothing <u>more disgusting</u> than a warthog.	That's not true! I'll bet <u>there are plenty of more disgusting creatures</u>.

7 **Listen.** How do the speakers express and respond to strong opinions? Write the phrases you hear. TR: 58

8 **Read and complete the dialogue.**

Rama: Hey Tina, I need your help. We're choosing an animal to represent the school's environmental club. What do you think?

Tina: Wow, some of the animals on this list are really ugly! Let's use a panda. _____ cuter than a panda.

Rama: _____ There are plenty of animals that are just as cute. And _____ there are more interesting animals. Look at this picture of an African warthog, for example.

A warthog

Tina: No way! _____ warthogs are the ugliest animals _____ . No one will want to join our club.

Rama: Really? I think they're _____ cool. They look so mean, but they're actually more likely to run away from a predator than to fight! And they can run really fast! A warthog would definitely make people look at our poster!

Tina: Yeah, but not in a good way. Here's an interesting animal: the axolotl. They're really cool because they never age. _____ cuter than pandas.

Rama: Yeah, they are pretty cute. OK, let's use the axolotl.

9 **Work in groups.** Toss a coin and move. (Heads = 1 space; tails = 2 spaces) Give and respond to strong opinions about the animal on each square.

10 **Work in pairs.** Discuss animals, people, things, and places that you think are unusual, interesting, or beautiful. Give strong opinions and listen as your partner responds. Then switch roles.

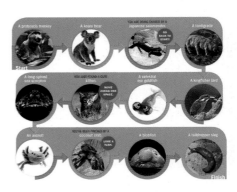

Go to p. 161.

Present perfect: Describing past experiences that connect to the present

I **have studied** many extreme environments, but **I've never been** to Antarctica.

The scientists **have already discovered** two new species, but they **haven't named** them **yet**.

Have you **ever seen** a giant tube worm?

The study of extremophiles **has taught** us a lot about the origins of life on Earth.

11 **Read.** Complete the paragraph with the present-perfect forms of the verbs in parentheses.

Kevin Hand wants to find out if there is life on Europa, one of Jupiter's moons. In his research, he _____ (travel) all around the world to study extremophiles in their different environments. He _____ (explore) northern Alaska, and he _____ (be) to the glaciers of Mount Kilimanjaro. He _____ (find) microbes at the bottom of the ocean. But, of course, he _____ (never/sail) on the frozen sea of Europa. _____ (he/ever/dream) of going into outer space? "Sure," says Kevin. "But the reality is that it will probably be another 15 years before a mission can explore Europa." And although Kevin _____ (not/visit/Europa/yet), he and his colleague Robert Carlson _____ (build) what they call "Europa-in-a-can." They _____ (create) conditions in their lab that are similar to those under the frozen sea of Europa. This will help them understand how organisms exist in this extreme environment.

12 **Work independently.** Write sentences using the present perfect.

1. coldest place / ever / be _The coldest place I've ever been is Moscow. It was −15° C!_

2. strangest animal / ever / see _____

3. most beautiful place / ever / go to _____

4. biggest animal / ever / touch _____

13 **Work in pairs.** Take turns asking and answering about your answers to Activity 12.

Europa

What's the coldest place you've ever been?

The coldest place I've ever been is Moscow.

14 **Learn new words.** Listen to learn about extremophiles and their environments. Then listen and repeat. TR: 60 and 61

Some extremophiles thrive in the **high-pressure** environment around hydrothermal vents. Although the environment above the sea is **normal** for us, the low pressure above water **kills** these extremophiles. When scientists bring them up to the **surface** of the sea, they can **die**.

Underwater hydrothermal vents

Extremophile environment

15 **Work independently.** Write a short paragraph on extremophiles. Describe their habitats and why scientists are interested in them. Use the words in the box.

condition	die	environment	kill
life	normal	pressure	thrive

_____

_____

_____

_____

_____

16 **Work in pairs.** Role-play an interview between a scientist studying extremophiles and a reporter who wants to feature them in a story. Include the following in your interview:

- extreme environments the scientist has visited
- information the scientist has learned
- gadgets the scientist has developed or used
- animals the scientist has studied/reported on

WEIRD
and Wonderful

Who says bizarre is bad?

Let's take a look at some of the more bizarre animals on our planet. Some people may think that these remarkable creatures are not as beautiful as cute little kittens or majestic lions. But that doesn't mean that they're not just as important. These fascinating creatures have a lot to teach us about the natural world.

The purple pig-nosed frog lives in India, and it is known for its strangely-shaped nose. This rare animal was only discovered in 2003 because it spends most of its time in a burrow several meters below the ground. It eats a diet of worms and other bugs. For about two weeks every year, during the heavy rain of the monsoons, the pig-nosed frog comes out of its burrow to breed. Then it goes back inside for the rest of the year.

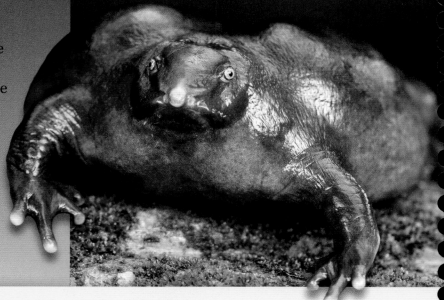

17 **Before you read, discuss in pairs.** Based on the title and the photos, what do you think the reading is about?

18 **Learn new words.** Find these words in the text. Look at the photos for clues about each word's meaning. Then listen and repeat. TR: 62

| bizarre | parasite | rare | tongue |

19 **While you read, notice what type of information is given about each animal.**
TR: 63

20 **After you read, work in pairs to answer these questions.**

1. Why did scientists only recently discover the purple pig-nosed frog?

2. Why does it come out of its burrow?

3. Where does the tongue-eating louse live?

4. What happens to the fish after the tongue-eating louse eats its tongue?

5. Why does the blobfish look so bizarre?

6. Why do we not have much information about it?

The tongue-eating louse is a tiny 8 mm (0.5 in.) parasite that lives in oceans throughout much of the world. A parasite survives by living on and feeding off of another creature. You can probably guess from its name that the tongue-eating louse eats tongues, specifically fish tongues. After it has eaten the tongue, the louse lives inside the fish's mouth. Amazingly, this doesn't kill the fish. Instead, the fish just starts to use the louse as a replacement tongue. It sounds frightening, but don't worry—the tongue-eating louse doesn't eat human tongues!

We don't know much about the extraordinary blobfish because it lives in very deep waters of the ocean between Tasmania and New Zealand. It doesn't have any muscles or bones, which is why it has such a strange appearance when it's on the surface of the sea. When it's in its natural habitat, it looks like a normal fish because the pressure of the water pushes its body into shape. No one has ever filmed the blobfish in its natural environment, but scientists believe that the blobfish doesn't swim. Instead, it just floats in the water and waits for fish and other sea animals to swim into its mouth.

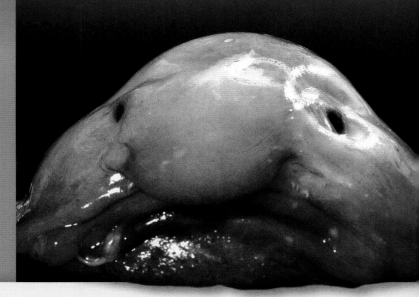

21 **Create a chart to organize information about each animal's habitat, diet, and appearance.** Complete the chart with information from the reading.

22 **Discuss in groups.**

1. Which of the three animals do you like best? Which do you like the least? Explain your answers.

2. What features make animals look attractive or beautiful? Do you think people care more about beautiful animals? Why or why not?

3. The blobfish has been chosen as the ugliest animal in the world! Does it deserve this title? Why or why not? If not, what animal does deserve it?

VIDE▶

23 **Before you watch, discuss in pairs.**

1. Look at the photo. What do you think it shows?

2. How do you think the photographer got this photo? What equipment did he use? What problems might he have had?

24 **Work in pairs.** Read the sentences below. Circle the one that you believe to be true, based on the photo.

1. The horsehair worm is a parasite that lives inside of the cricket.

2. The cricket is a parasite that lives inside of the horsehair worm.

3. The horsehair worm is a predator that hunts crickets.

4. Crickets and horsehair worms are never together.

25 Watch scene 5.1. **While you watch, take notes on how Anand Varma photographs the cricket and the horsehair worm.**

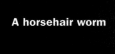

A horsehair worm

26 **After you watch, work in pairs.** Decide if these sentences are *true* or *false.* Check the correct answer.

1. Most of the photos that Anand had seen of parasites were very beautiful.　　**T**　**F**

2. Anand wants to make people think that parasites are cool.　　**T**　**F**

3. To get the photograph, Anand puts the cricket into water with a special mixture of salts.　　**T**　**F**

4. Anand thought it was easy to photograph the cricket and the horsehair worm.　　**T**　**F**

5. Putting the animals in salt water made it more difficult for Anand to photograph them.　　**T**　**F**

6. Anand feels that every job he has gives him a new challenge.　　**T**　**F**

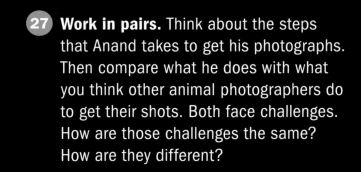

A cricket

27 **Work in pairs.** Think about the steps that Anand takes to get his photographs. Then compare what he does with what you think other animal photographers do to get their shots. Both face challenges. How are those challenges the same? How are they different?

28 **Work in groups.** Anand is creating a graphic novel to show how parasites live. Research another parasite. Then create a page of a graphic novel to show how that parasite interacts with its host. Include several panels to show how the relationship changes over time.

29 **Choose an activity.**

1. **Work independently.** Find an animal photo that you really like. It could be a photo that you took, or one taken by a friend, family member, or a photographer. Write a description of the photo, explaining why you like it and how it was taken.

2. **Work in pairs.** Choose a parasite and learn about how it survives. Then write a short skit about the relationship between the parasite and its host. Perform your skit for the class.

3. **Work in groups.** At the beginning of the video, Anand says, "People tend to not like parasites very much." Discuss in groups why that is. Do you think a parasite is better than a predator, such as a lion? Why or why not? Share your discussion with the class.

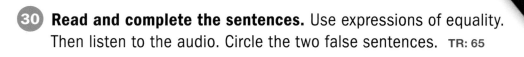

GRAMMAR TR: 64

A Pacific hagfish

As . . . as: Making comparisons of equality

The Pacific hagfish is just **as important as** other fish.

Polar bears can't swim **as fast as** penguins.

The blue whale weighs **as much as** 23 elephants!

Humans have **as many hairs on their bodies as** chimpanzees.

30 **Read and complete the sentences.** Use expressions of equality. Then listen to the audio. Circle the two false sentences. TR: 65

1. The Pacific hagfish is just _____ (unusual) many of the other animals you've learned about.

2. The hagfish is around 300 million years old: about _____ (old) the first land animals.

3. The hagfish has only lived _____ (long) the dinosaurs.

4. The hagfish has evolved _____ (much) all other animals.

5. The hagfish can swim 1,675 m (5,500 ft.) below the surface of the sea. That's _____ (deep) the blobfish can swim!

31 **Read.** Write sentences using expressions of equality.

1. I think blobfish and naked mole rats are both very ugly.

   I think blobfish are as ugly as naked mole rats.

2. An adult warthog and a baby elephant both weigh around 90 kg (200 lb.).

   _____

3. Proboscis monkeys and snow leopards are both endangered. According to some estimates, there are only about 7,000 of each left in the world.

   _____

4. The frilled shark swims deep in the ocean, at 1,500 m (5,000 ft.) below the surface. That's also where the Pacific hagfish swims.

   _____

32 **Work in groups.** Survey your classmates for two minutes. Find classmates who have things in common with you. Write their names in the spaces provided. When time is up, report back to your group.

> I wake up as early as Juan and Lea.

Category	Me	People similar to me
Wake-up time	6:00	Juan Lea

88

Go to p. 163.

In persuasive writing, we must support our point of view with facts. To connect our ideas, we can use transitional phrases like:

as a result (of)   **because**   **for this/these reason(s)**   **therefore**

33 **Read the model.** Work in pairs to identify how the writer connects ideas. Underline the words and phrases.

Save the Axolotl!

The axolotl is an endangered animal. It lives in Mexico now, but scientists believe that it could be extinct in the wild in five to ten years. However, it isn't as attractive as other endangered animals, like giant pandas or Siberian tigers. As a result, it doesn't get very much attention.

The axolotl has an amazing ability: if it loses a part of its body, it can grow it back. For example, if another animal bites off an axolotl's leg, it grows a new leg! Scientists are studying the axolotl because they want to learn how its cells can do this. This research might lead scientists to help humans with damaged body parts.

Another interesting fact about the axolotl is that it never becomes an adult. Other amphibians, like frogs, change from being a tadpole into a frog. But the axolotl is always an adolescent. For this reason, scientists believe that we can find out about the secret of aging from the axolotl.

There is also a cultural reason to save the axolotl. In Aztec legends, the axolotl was a great god and he changed into an animal to hide from death. Therefore, if this creature becomes extinct, an important link with Aztec culture will be lost forever.

For all of the above reasons, we should do everything possible to save this fascinating creature.

34 **Work in pairs.** Why should we protect the axolotl? Give three reasons.

35 **Write.** Write a persuasive essay. Choose another unusual endangered animal. Persuade your readers to protect it.

Ask Questions

"Ask questions no matter how intimidating it might seem. The exciting side of science really resides in the questions."

—Kevin Hand

National Geographic Explorer, Planetary Scientist/Astrobiologist

1. **Watch scene 5.2.**

2. Write a list of questions about how animals and plants survive in your area. How can you find the answers to these questions?

3. Choose one of the animals featured in this unit, and find out more about it. What type of environment does it live in? How does it handle the conditions in its environment? Could it live in your area? Why or why not?

Make an Impact

A **Create a brochure for a conservation organization.**

- Research several unusual creatures that are endangered. Collect information and photos about the animals.
- Create a brochure for a conservation organization. Explain why these animals are threatened and why it's important to save them.
- Design a logo for the front of the brochure. Share your completed brochure with the class.

B **Plan and hold a contest for the best "survivor."**

- Work in groups to choose at least five animals that have interesting or unusual survival skills.
- Present the animals to the class. Show photos and explain what each animal does to survive in its environment.
- Have a class vote to decide the best survivor of the group.

C **Write a journal entry.**

- Choose an extreme environment, and imagine that you explore it.
- Write a journal entry about your journey. Describe why you're taking it, what equipment you need, and what you discover.
- Read your journal entry aloud in class. Answer your classmates' questions.

The sand cat lives in the extreme heat of the desert. It doesn't need water to survive.

Are You Going to Eat That?

"I would encourage everyone who sees a food and thinks it's weird to try it once. And then they'd probably try it again."

—Tristram Stuart

Misshaped carrots

1. Look at the photo. Would you eat these? Why or why not?

2. When is the last time you tried a completely new type of food? What was it? Did you enjoy it or not?

3. What's your favorite food? Has the type of food you like changed as you've gotten older? Explain, with examples.

Look at the photo. Where is the food? Why might it be there?
Discuss. Then listen and read. TR: 66

Think about the last time you visited a **supermarket**. Did you see any short, fat carrots? Were all the bananas in the bunch different **sizes**? And were there any strange lumps on the potatoes? If you answered "no" to these questions, there's a reason why. Supermarkets in many parts of the world set very high **standards** for the **appearance** of their fruits and vegetables. Many supermarket employees believe that **consumers** want everything to look perfect. But if supermarkets reject these unusual carrots and lumpy potatoes, what happens to them? They often go rotten in the **fields** or go into the dumpster, and from there, into **landfills**. In the United Kingdom alone, between 20 and 40 percent of fruits and vegetables are rejected before they even reach the stores.

It's a **shocking** statistic, but there are solutions to the problems of food **waste**. Author and activist Tristram Stuart organizes **campaigns** around the world called *Feeding the 5000*. At these events, people use food that would have otherwise gone to waste to prepare free, delicious meals for

5,000 people. Volunteers make good meals from fruits and vegetables that may not be pretty, but are still **nutritious** and fresh. In many cities, there are also *Disco Soup* parties. At these events, volunteers prepare meals from unwanted **produce** while they dance to music played by a DJ. These events are a lot of fun, and they make people think twice about throwing food away!

Some supermarkets are also trying to get people to think differently. The French supermarket chain *Intermarché* **supplies** ugly food in its stores. The fruits and vegetables look strange, but they're **edible**.

They're also less expensive than more attractive produce. Consumers love the idea. In fact, *Intermarché* stores sold more than 1,200 kg (2,645 lb.) of ugly fruits and vegetables in the first two days of the campaign.

So what can you do? Start by eating what's on your plate! And don't be afraid to try ugly or unusual foods. You can even organize a food waste **challenge** for your friends and family! By telling people about the problem, you're working toward the solution.

Tristram Stuart at a *Feeding the 5000* event in Trafalgar Square, London

2 **Learn new words.** Listen and repeat. TR: 67

3 **Work in pairs.** Do you waste food at school or at home? If so, how much? Why would you throw food away?

4 **Read and write the words from the list.**

campaign	edible	landfill	nutritious
produce	shocking	supply	waste

Tristram Stuart first became interested in the issue of food _____
when he was a teenager. He kept a few pigs, and he would feed them with unwanted food.
Local bakers, grocers, and even his school cafeteria would _____ food
for him to feed his pigs. He also used _____ that he found in trash cans
behind the supermarket. He soon realized that these fruits and vegetables were actually tasty,
_____ , and perfectly _____ for humans. There
was no reason why they couldn't be eaten. The _____ amount of food in
the trash inspired Tristram to start a _____ to inform people about the
issue and try to create change.

5 **Learn new words.** Listen for these words and match them to the definitions.
Then listen and repeat. **TR: 68 and 69**

fresh	to reject	rotten	to throw away

_____ 1. not accept something

_____ 2. put something in the trash

_____ 3. recently produced or picked

_____ 4. no longer edible

6 **Choose an activity.**

1. **Work independently.** Write a letter
   to your principal. Explain why food
   waste is a problem, and make two
   suggestions for how waste can be
   reduced at your school.

2. **Work in pairs.** Imagine your local
   supermarket wants to start an ugly
   fruit and vegetable campaign. Create
   a poster for their campaign.

3. **Work in groups.** Imagine you want
   to open a restaurant. How can you
   avoid food waste? Make a list of at
   least five ideas.

Farmers cut green beans to supermarket standards. As a
result, 40 percent of their crops are thrown away.

7 **Listen.** How do the speakers ask for repetition and repeat information? Write the phrases you hear. TR: 71

8 **Read and complete the dialogue.**

Kyoko: Hey, listen up, everyone. I want to tell you about this Disco Soup event that Jun and I went to last weekend.

Haku: I'm sorry, I _____ you said. Miso soup?

Kyoko: No, not *miso* soup. What _____ *Disco* Soup. It's an event where people get together to prepare soup from unwanted food, while listening to music.

Sakura: Excuse me, but _____ please? Did you just say that you prepare soup and listen to music at the same time?

Kyoko: That's right! And we use food that the supermarkets reject because of shape or size.

Haku: Sorry? _____ that. Where does the food come from?

Kyoko: I just _____ we use food that the supermarkets reject. So all the food is free.

Sakura: Free? That's amazing!

Kyoko: I know! Maybe we can organize a Disco Soup event here at school. What do you think?

Haku: Sounds good to me!

9 **Work in large groups.** Cut out the cards and use them to play "Telephone." Speak as quietly as possible. If you don't hear what your group member says, ask for repetition.

10 **Work in groups.** Play the game in Activity 9 again, this time with your own topics.

Sorry? I didn't catch that.

No problem. What I said was that each year, 1.3 billion tons of edible food is wasted worldwide.

Each year, 1.3 billion tons of edible food is wasted worldwide.

Go to p. 165.

97

Going to, will, and present progressive:
Talking about the future

I'm **going to start** making my own lunches.

Are you **going to try** this food?

I think we **will buy** more ugly food in the future.

My brother probably **won't eat** this because it looks strange.

What's the cafeteria **serving** for lunch tomorrow?

I'm **speaking** to the director about our school's food waste at 3:00.

11 **Listen.** Then circle the correct letter, based on what you hear. TR: 73

1.	a. I'm meeting	b. I'm going to meet
2.	a. We're helping	b. We will help
3.	a. We're preparing	b. We're going to prepare
4.	a. Are you going to be	b. Will you be
5.	a. I will spend	b. I'm going to spend
6.	a. We're going to serve	b. We're serving
7.	a. I'm calling	b. I'm going to call
8.	a. We won't waste	b. We aren't wasting

12 **Work in pairs.** Discuss your answers to the questions below.

1. You have a bag of soft apples. What are you going to do with them?

2. What are you eating for dinner tonight? Will you eat it all?

3. You don't like what's in your lunchbox. What are you going to do?

4. You want to make a smoothie. What kinds of fruit are you going to use?

5. What will you do to help change people's ideas about food waste?

> I'm going to make apple pie with them.

> Great idea! I'm going to use them to make apple juice.

13 **Work in pairs.** Discuss future plans. Use the phrases in the box.

in fifty years	**in the future**	**later today**
next weekend	**tomorrow**	**tonight**

> What are you doing later today?

> I'm watching the game with my dad.

14 **Learn new words.** Listen to learn how to prepare a meal with leftover food. Then listen and repeat. **TR: 74 and 75**

to chop

to fry

to boil

to mash

to bake

Shepherd's pie

15 **Work in pairs.** Write three different foods on a piece of paper. Exchange your paper with another pair. Come up with a way to prepare each of the foods on the new list. Describe each meal and how you will prepare it.

> We're preparing fried eggplant with tomato sauce. First, we're going to fry the eggplant . . .

16 **Work in groups.** Plan three meals for your cafeteria to serve next week. Talk about how you'll prepare each meal. Then survey your classmates to see which of your lunch options will be the most popular. Share your plan and the survey results with the class.

> We're going to prepare pizza, turkey sandwiches, and carrot soup. On the first day, we're baking pizzas. We'll start by chopping the vegetables . . .

Before you read, work in pairs.
Scan the text for numbers. What
information do you think they give?

18 **Learn new words.** Find these words
in the text. Which two words are
antonyms? Use a dictionary to check.
Then listen and repeat. TR: 76

| decision | to decrease | to increase |
| to involve | to rush | |

19 **While you read, underline the
numbers in the text.** TR: 77

20 **After you read, look at the
sentences.** Check T for *true* and
F for *false*.

1. Students waste less
   food if their lunch time
   is longer. (T) (F)

2. When recess is after
   lunch, students eat more. (T) (F)

3. Students don't want to
   make decisions about
   their school menu. (T) (F)

4. Some schools get their
   food from charities. (T) (F)

21 **Complete the sentences.**

1. Lunch in US schools is usually

   between _____ and _____
   minutes long.

2. If recess is before lunch, schools

   reduce plate waste by _____ percent.

3. Students put _____ percent of their
   school lunch into the trash.

4. Longer lunch breaks reduce food

   waste by _____ .

Clean Your Plate!

Cafeteria Waste and What Can Be Done About It

It's lunchtime. You rush into the
school cafeteria. You've only got 20 minutes
to eat, but you also want time to relax with
your friends before afternoon classes. So you
quickly get some food, eat half of it, and then
the bell rings. What happens to the rest of the
food on your tray? Chances are, it goes right
into the trash.

Does this sound familiar? Even if you don't
do this, you probably know someone who does.
In fact, in the United States, nearly a third of the
food served in school cafeterias goes into the
trash. All that wasted food is worth nearly one
billion US dollars every year.

Although food waste is a problem, many
schools are finding ways to decrease the
amount of food that gets thrown away. Some
have simply changed when lunch is served.
Students often rush to finish their food so that
they can go to recess. But when recess is before
lunch, students get the chance to burn off some
energy first. Then they're hungry and ready
to eat.

Do you have much time for lunch? If you're
like many students, you probably don't. Short
lunch breaks make many students rush. When
students don't have time to eat, they are more
likely to throw food away. Schools with longer
lunch hours have less waste.

Around **30%** of food served in US school cafeterias is wasted.

When recess is before lunch, waste decreases by as much as **30%.**

If schools increase the lunch break from **20 to 30 minutes,** students throw away one-third less food.

Some schools are trying to involve students more and get them to make decisions about the food in their school. For example, some US schools reduced cafeteria waste by 36 percent when students could choose what food the cafeteria served. In many schools, students can make suggestions about the menu and then give their feedback later. It's also helpful to let students serve themselves. This way, they only take what they think they'll eat. Getting students involved can make a big difference.

Even with all these great ideas, there will always be some food waste. However, all the unwanted food doesn't have to go into the landfill. Some charities collect unwanted food from schools and use it to feed hungry people. One UK school came up with a great idea—Fruity Friday. Each Friday, students chop up all the leftover fruit from the cafeteria and use it to make special desserts for the whole school. And of course, fruits and vegetables can be composted, or left to break down. Compost can then be used to make soil healthier and grow more produce.

How much food is wasted at your school? What can you do to change the situation?

22 **Discuss in groups.**

1. Why do you think the length of time for lunch is important? How much time do you get for lunch? How long does it take you to eat?

2. Think about how you could change your school's cafeteria to encourage students to eat all their lunch. Discuss the design of the cafeteria, the different places where students can eat, and the way food is presented.

3. The reading mentions several different solutions to the problem of food waste at school. Think of another solution. Think about both how to stop food waste before it starts and what can be done with the unwanted food.

VIDEO ▶

23 **Before you watch, discuss in pairs.** Look at the strawberries in the photo. Do they look like the strawberries you usually eat? If not, what's different about them?

24 **Work in pairs.** You're going to watch a video called *What Makes Food Appealing?* Before you watch, discuss this question. Then think of what makes food unappealing to you.

25 Watch scene 6.1. **While you watch, answer the questions.** What three things can make our food appealing? Which of them is most important to you?

26 **After you watch, work in pairs to answer the questions.**

1. What is a food stylist?

2. What are two examples of how food stylists make food look good?

3. What happens to produce if it isn't the right size, color, or shape for some supermarkets?

4. Why do some people feel better about buying food directly from farmers?

5. What's the difference between how supermarkets sell their produce and how farmers sell their produce?

6. What do farmers often do with the food that they can't sell?

27 **Work in pairs.** Do you think it's OK to change the way food looks so that it's more appealing in advertisements? Why or why not?

28 **Discuss in groups.** Does advertising sometimes persuade you to visit certain stores or try certain foods? Which advertisements do you think are the most persuasive? Why are they successful?

29 Choose an activity.

1. **Work independently.** Find an advertisement for a food product in a newspaper or magazine. Write a paragraph about it. Explain how the advertisement makes the food look appealing.

2. **Work in pairs.** Choose a food product, and create an advertisement for it. Think about how you can make the food look and sound as appealing as possible.

3. **Work in groups.** Compare farmers' markets with supermarkets. Include information about the look, taste, and origin of the foods sold at each place. Present your comparison to the class.

Conditionals: Talking about cause and effect

If you're hungry, **don't buy** extra food.
If there's food in your kitchen, **eat** that instead.

If we **make** a smoothie from these old bananas, it **will be** delicious.

If food **looks** bad, we **throw** it away.

If you **don't eat** this lunch, it **will go** into the landfill.

30 **Read.** Match the phrases to form logical sentences. Write the letter.

_____ 1. If you don't finish your sandwich,   a. you will waste less food.

_____ 2. If you find some old carrots,   b. put some in the freezer for later.

_____ 3. If you have some leftover chicken,   c. think of a way to make it taste better.

_____ 4. If you don't like this vegetable,   d. you can take the rest for lunch tomorrow.

_____ 5. If you cook too much food,   e. make them into soup.

_____ 6. If you learn more about cooking,   f. it will be good in a sandwich.

31 **Work in pairs.** Write your own endings to these sentences.

1. If my school serves pasta for lunch tomorrow, _____

_____

2. If we talk more about food waste, _____

_____

3. If I prepare dinner for my family tonight, _____

_____

4. If you give your lunch to another student, _____

_____

5. If we go to the supermarket this weekend, _____

_____

6. If we don't cook food properly, _____

_____

32 **Work in pairs.** Take turns. Use a coin to move. (Heads = 1 space; tails = 2 spaces) Create sentences with conditionals.

If you don't like green peppers, don't buy them!

Go to p. 167.

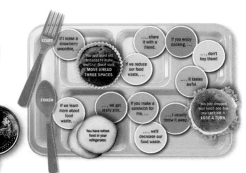

When we write to explain, we often describe causes and effects. To do this, we can use the following phrases:

as a result (of)   **because (of)**   **for this reason/these reasons**   **that's why**

33 **Read the model.** Work in pairs to identify how the writer signals cause and effect. Underline the phrases.

We waste 1.3 billion tons of food every year. This is too much wasted food. There are millions of people that don't have enough to eat. Food waste isn't just bad for humans, though. It's also bad for the environment.

When we put food waste into the landfill, it produces a dangerous gas that can keep heat inside of the Earth's atmosphere. That's why it's one of the causes of global warming. There are also chemicals that come out of the food and go into the soil. When it rains, the chemicals then go into our rivers and canals. As a result, food waste harms our bodies of water.

People don't think about how food is made when they're throwing it away. A lot of water is used to grow plants that make food. We use a lot of energy because we need fuel to transport food from the field to the supermarket, and then to our homes. If we waste this food, we waste our planet's natural resources.

For these reasons, it is important for us all to reduce our food waste.

34 **Work in pairs.** The writer shows that wasting food is harmful to the environment. What are the three causes of environmental harm mentioned by the writer?

35 **Write.** Why do people throw food away? Write about at least three different causes of food waste.

Take Only What You Need

"The solution is as simple as eating and enjoying food rather than throwing it away."

—Tristram Stuart

National Geographic Explorer, Author and Campaigner

1. **Watch scene 6.2.**

2. Make a log of all the food you waste at home for a week. Make a list of at least three changes that you will make to waste less food in the future.

3. In what situations do you take more than you need? Think about food, as well as other things. Why do you do it? Why is it important to take only what you need?

Make an Impact

A **Create a recipe book.**

· Find out about what food is wasted at your school and at home.

· Look for recipes to use this unwanted food.

· Compile the recipes into a book. Share your recipe book with the class.

B **Write an article about waste in your community.**

· Interview workers at a local restaurant, café, or supermarket about their experience with food waste.

· Take notes during your interview. Include statistics about food waste. Talk about steps that are being taken to decrease waste.

· Write a short magazine article about the problem. Suggest solutions in your article.

C **Create a comic strip about food waste.**

· Choose foods to be the characters of your comic strip. Create a dialogue in which the foods talk about how being thrown in the trash makes them feel.

· Draw your comic strip, and include your dialogue.

· Make copies of your comic strip to share with the class.

Express Yourself

1 **Read and listen to the story.** TR: 79

A New Beginning

It's another day on Alteron 5. Another long, uneventful day. Outside, the sunrise fills the sky with a deep blue light. I check the information on my screen. Oxygen levels are good. Temperature in here is 20°C (68°F). Temperature outside is 40°C (104°F). Engine is dead. Food levels are low. I have enough food now for maybe one more month, if I move slowly and sleep a lot. How long have I been here? Six months? A year? Two years? Time works differently when a day lasts 50 hours. I lost communication weeks ago. Now the only voice I hear is the one in my head.

Slowly I put on my heavy suit, my helmet, my boots, my safety harness. One more journey around the vehicle. One more check. Maybe I've missed something. Maybe this time the engine will suddenly come back to life. Outside, into the heat I go. Check the doors. Check the wings. Check the engine. I step over some rocks. I pick up an empty water bottle I must have dropped. Then I stop. Look again. I see something strange on the ground. There, where I put my last apple core. A tiny stem, with something strange and ugly at the end of it. Small, blue, and lumpy. Could this be a new beginning?

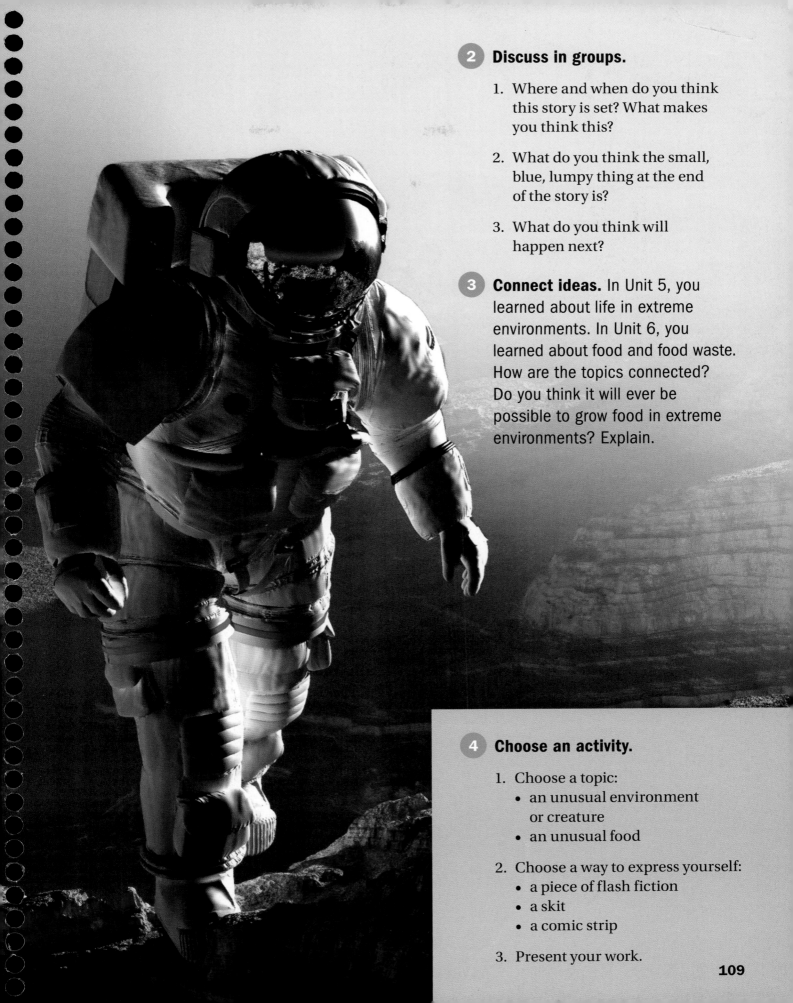

2 Discuss in groups.

1. Where and when do you think this story is set? What makes you think this?

2. What do you think the small, blue, lumpy thing at the end of the story is?

3. What do you think will happen next?

3 Connect ideas. In Unit 5, you learned about life in extreme environments. In Unit 6, you learned about food and food waste. How are the topics connected? Do you think it will ever be possible to grow food in extreme environments? Explain.

4 Choose an activity.

1. Choose a topic:
   • an unusual environment or creature
   • an unusual food

2. Choose a way to express yourself:
   • a piece of flash fiction
   • a skit
   • a comic strip

3. Present your work.

109

Art in the Open

"Art in the public space is meant to create a conversation. It's meant to challenge preconceptions. It's meant to inspire."
—Shannon Galpin

Houses painted to create a mural in the *Las Palmitas* neighborhood of Pachuca, Mexico

1. Look at the photo. Do you like what you see? Do you think it's art? Why or why not?

2. What are the differences between art in a gallery and art in the street or in a park? Where do you prefer to look at art?

3. Think of a piece of artwork or photograph you love. Describe it and explain why you love it.

111

1 **Where can you see art?** Discuss. Then listen and read. TR: 80

When you hear the word *art*, you probably think of paintings in galleries or **statues** in museums. But art isn't always inside, and you don't always have to pay to see it. In fact, you can **view** some really interesting art for **free** in **public spaces** around the world.

Public art goes beyond just making a place look pretty: it can change society. In Las Palmitas, a neighborhood of Pachuca, Mexico, residents worked together with a street art group to paint their hillside houses in bright colors. The result was an enormous mural that can be seen from miles away. As the community worked together on the project, they noticed how the art brought joy to their neighborhood. "In the morning, you wake up and look around and see the colors that **surround** you," said one resident. "It's very pretty."

Public art can also send a message. For example, much public art **deals with** political and **social topics**. In 2014, British artists Paul Cummins and Tom Piper placed 888,246 ceramic poppies on the ground around the Tower of London. The **temporary** display of artwork was in honor of the hundred-year anniversary of the start of World War I. Each poppy represented a soldier who died in the war while fighting with the British. The goal was for visitors to think about and **remember** the soldiers. After several months, the artwork was **taken down**, and the poppies were sold to raise money for charity.

Public art can also make people **aware** of a situation. In 2010, the Icelandic artist Bjargey Ólafsdóttir created *Red Polar Bear* on the Langjökull glacier in Iceland. It **showed** the red outline of a polar bear on the snow. The very large bear—80 m (262 ft.) by 50 m (164 ft.)—was made out of red food dye. Ólafsdóttir wanted to make people think about the polar bear and how its environment is in danger because of global warming.

Of course, sometimes public art is there simply because its beauty brings people **pleasure**. One example is the *Floralis Genérica* in Buenos Aires, a huge metal flower in a pool. It opens every morning and closes every evening. The flower and the pool reflect everything around them. It's an amazing sight.

Red Polar Bear (2010) by Bjargey Ólafsdóttir

2 Learn new words. Listen and repeat.
TR: 81

3 Work in pairs. Why do people create public art? What do you think is the most important reason for creating it?

113

4 **Read and write the words from the list.** Make any necessary changes.

aware	deal with	free	public space	show
social	surround	take down	topic	view

Adventurer and humanitarian Shannon Galpin wanted to make people

_____ of what life is like in Afghanistan. She organized an exhibition

of photographs called *Streets of Afghanistan*. The photographs _____

the people of Afghanistan in their daily lives and _____ many

different _____ , from shopping and playing sports to homelessness

and poverty. The exhibition first opened in Denver, Colorado, in the United States.

Shannon later decided to take the photographs to Afghanistan. She put up huge prints of

the photographs in _____

in Afghanistan, such as the streets or the zoo.

There, they were _____

for everyone to look at. People stopped to

_____ them as they walked

through the streets.

Shannon Galpin and the *Streets of Afghanistan* exhibition

5 **Learn new words.** Listen for these words and match them to the definitions. Then listen and repeat. **TR: 82 and 83**

joy	mural	political	society

_____ 1. a large painting on a wall

_____ 2. people living in an organized group

_____ 3. a feeling of great happiness

_____ 4. related to the government or laws of a country

6 **Choose an activity.**

1. **Work independently.** Imagine you're a photographer. Find photos that represent your country. Show them to the class, and explain what they say about your country and its people.

2. **Work in pairs.** Find out more about Shannon Galpin's *Streets of Afghanistan* project. What do you think of it? Would you like to see an exhibition like this focusing on your country? Why or why not?

3. **Work in groups.** Imagine you want to use a public space for an art show. What kind of space will you use? What do you want to show in it? Discuss your ideas.

SPEAKING STRATEGY TR: 84

Asking for more information

What's it like?

How <u>big/wide/high/long</u> is it?

Who <u>created/designed/painted</u> it?

Where is it?

How was it <u>built/transported/put up</u>?

A statue of Hachikō the dog, joyfully greeting his owner

7 **Listen.** How do the speakers ask for more information? Write the phrases you hear. TR: 85

8 **Read and complete the dialogue.**

Jay: How was your weekend in Chicago?

Yasmin: It was great. I think the best thing was this amazing video sculpture I saw.

Jay: _____

Yasmin: It's really interesting. There are two huge towers at each end of a pool. Video screens on the towers show people spitting water into the pool.

Jay: _____ are the towers?

Yasmin: They're about 15 m (50 ft.) high.

Jay: Wow, that's big! _____

Yasmin: It was designed by a Spanish artist, Jaume Plensa.

Jay: _____

Yasmin: It's in Millennium Park. You should go see it if you're ever in Chicago.

9 **Work in groups.** Pick two information cards. Then pick one photo card. Ask your group members about the piece of art on the photo card. Give details when someone asks about the artwork on your information cards.

10 **Work in pairs.** Imagine that you have a plan for a piece of public art. Tell your partner about it. Describe its size, location, and what it will look like. Then ask questions to find out about your partner's art.

Jelly Baby Family
- Seven brightly-colored figures
- Daddy Jelly Baby is 1.9 m (6 ft.) tall, weighs 350 kg (770 lb.)
- Also a mother and three children
- Artist: Mauro Perucchetti
- Location: Singapore

Go to p. 169.

115

Simple past vs. present perfect: Talking about the past

Shannon Galpin **has biked** in many different countries. In 2009, she **went** to Afghanistan.

Has she **ever made** a movie? Yes, she **has**. She **made** a movie called *Afghan Cycles* in 2014. **Have** you **seen** it **yet**?

She **has worked** on art projects in Afghanistan **since** 2010. She **organized** the *Streets of Afghanistan* exhibition in 2013.

11 **Read.** Choose the best option to complete the sentences.

came	created	has been	have ever seen	has made	have never run into	sat

What's the weirdest sculpture you _____? I bet you

_____ a giant yellow rabbit in the middle of the street! In 2011, Dutch

artist Florentijn Hofman _____ a 13 m (42 ft.) statue of a yellow toy

rabbit in Örebro, Sweden. And Hofman is not the only artist who _____

giant statues of toys. Urs Fischer's statue *Untitled (lamp/bear)* _____ in

a New York City plaza for five months in 2011. In Tokyo, a 20 m (65 ft.) plastic robot, *Gundam*,

_____ a popular tourist attraction since 2009. In fact, 4.5 million visitors

_____ to see the robot in a single month.

12 **Work independently.** Listen and find out about artist Yue Minjun. Then use the words in the box to write a short description of Yue and his art. TR: 87

1992	2007	$6 million	around the world	at night
electrician	laughing face	paint	sculpture	understand

_____

_____

_____

_____

_____

_____

_____

_____

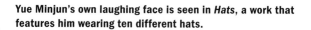

Yue Minjun's own laughing face is seen in *Hats*, a work that
features him wearing ten different hats.

Candy Chang's *Before I Die* walls are a **simple** way for people to **express themselves**. Some people write **fun** messages, but others want to say something more **serious**.

14 Work in pairs. What would you write on the *Before I Die* wall? Write your message and describe it to your partner.

Before I die, _____

_____

_____

15 Discuss in groups.

1. Chang's project uses a very simple idea to get people to express themselves. Think of another simple way to do this.

2. How have you used art to express yourself in the past? Give one or two examples.

3. Name one fun thing and one serious thing you've never done but would like to do.

4. Describe one piece of art that you've already seen and would like to see again.

The City That Loves

How Rio de Janeiro transformed its streets

If you walk through the streets of Rio de Janeiro, Brazil, you'll immediately notice something extraordinary about the city: the street art. All around the city, the walls are covered in colorful murals and bright paintings. In the past, this street art was illegal. But in 2009, the city passed a law allowing street art on private buildings if the owner gives permission. In 2014, Rio de Janeiro became the first city in the world to legalize graffiti in places such as skate parks and the walls that surround construction sites.

People who want to create street art in Rio de Janeiro can't just paint any wall with any picture, though. They still have to respect some rules. Street art and graffiti are legal, but just signing a name on a wall is not. And if an artist wants to create a picture on the walls of someone's house or shop, the artist must ask the owner first. But getting permission might not be too hard. Street art is very popular throughout the city, both with the residents and with visitors. Many tourists come to Brazil just to see it. They can even take special guided street-art tours through Rio de Janeiro. The city's mayor has also set up a special online street-art project. Volunteers can join the project and travel around the city, taking photos

16 **Before you read, discuss in pairs.** Based on the title and the photo, what do you think the reading is about?

17 **Learn new words.** Find these words in the reading. What do you think they mean? Look for clues in the text to explain each word's meaning. Then listen and repeat. TR: 90

| graffiti | illegal |
| permission | to respect |

18 **While you read, think about the main idea of the reading.** TR: 91

19 **After you read, work in pairs to answer these questions.**

1. What's unusual about Rio de Janeiro?
2. What became legal in 2009?
3. Give examples of places where graffiti is legal in Rio.
4. What is the purpose of the street-art website?
5. How have street artists helped certain communities?

Street Art

An artist paints a mural during a street art festival in Rio de Janeiro.

of the street art. They then upload their photos onto a street-art website, along with other details, such as the location and the artist. This means that when someone paints a new piece of art over an old picture, there is still a record of what was there before.

In some communities, street artists have set up art schools and organized festivals to teach young people more about their art. They have even worked together with the police to paint murals on the walls. Street art in Rio de Janeiro has not only made the streets more colorful and exciting, it has also helped to bring communities together.

20 **Work in pairs.** What's the main idea of this reading? Underline the correct answer. Then check the other details that are mentioned.

☐ Some of the laws about street art in Rio

☐ Details of different street-art projects

☐ A description of the positive effects of street art in Rio

☐ A discussion about the pros and cons of street art

☐ Ways that tourists can enjoy street art in Rio

☐ A description of some of Rio's most famous street art

21 **Discuss in groups.**

1. What do you think of when you look at the street art in the photo? Do you like it? Would you like to see art like this outside of your home or school?

2. Imagine that you want to create street art. What images will you use, and how will you use them? What message will your art have?

3. What places should never be covered with street art? Why?

22 **Before you watch, discuss in pairs.**

1. Where do you usually look at photographs? What are they of?
2. What type of photography interests you? Why? How do you feel when you look at it?

23 **Work in pairs.** You are going to watch a video called *Streets of Afghanistan*. What do you know about Afghanistan?

24 Watch scene 7.1. **While you watch, notice how the Afghan people respond to the photos.** Check the emotions they show in the video:

☐ anger   ☐ fear

☐ boredom   ☐ interest

☐ curiosity   ☐ joy

☐ excitement   ☐ sadness

25 **After you watch, work in pairs.** Circle the correct option to complete the sentences.

1. Shannon first had the idea of putting on this photo display four *years / months* before the video was made.
2. Shannon hopes it's inspiring for little kids to *be in a beautiful place / see their country in a beautiful way.*
3. The man at the zoo says that he was *surprised by / not interested in* the photos.
4. Shannon says that some of the photos are beautiful, but also make you *afraid / think.*
5. The Afghan woman says that people can *create / learn* something from these photos.
6. Shannon believes that projects based in *hope / war* should be in Afghanistan.

This photo of a man with headphones is from the *Streets of Afghanistan* exhibition.

26 **Work in groups.** In the video, Shannon takes a collection of photos around Afghanistan and shows them to people in different regions. What kinds of difficulties do you think she experienced while doing this?

27 **Work in pairs.** Discuss the purpose of public art. What are the different reasons someone might decide to organize a public art project? What kinds of responses would they hope for? How might this be different from an art project in a museum or a gallery?

28 **Choose an activity.**

1. **Work independently.** Look at the photo on this page. Write a short story inspired by the photo.

2. **Work in pairs.** Shannon talks about art inviting a conversation. Look at the photo on this page. What questions do you want to ask about it? Why do you think she chose this photo for her show?

3. **Work in groups.** Think of a group of people in the world who are experiencing major problems. What kind of public art project do you think might be effective in helping them? Share your ideas with the class.

GRAMMAR TR: 92

Indefinite pronouns: Talking about people, places, and things without giving details

Someone has painted a mural on the wall of our school. I think it's great, but not **everyone** loves it.

If you can't think of **anywhere** to visit this weekend and you've got **nothing** else to do, why not come to the arts festival? You can see public art exhibitions **everywhere**.

	every	**some**	**any**	**no**
one	everyone	someone	anyone	no one
where	everywhere	somewhere	anywhere	nowhere
thing	everything	something	anything	nothing

29 **Work in pairs.** Choose the correct option to complete each sentence. Then discuss the sentences together. Do you agree with them?

1. I don't think *anyone / someone* should paint on public buildings without permission.

2. Public art should be *everywhere / nowhere* for people to enjoy.

3. *No one / Anyone* should have to pay to see art in a gallery.

4. Some people think we should spend public money on *anything / something* other than art, such as education.

30 **Read.** Complete the text with the correct indefinite pronoun.

Floralis Genérica, Buenos Aires, Argentina

You can find public art _____: in parks, town squares, outside important buildings, and even in the middle of the street! But not _____ loves it. In fact, public art can often be controversial. When _____ creates a new piece of art in a public space, it can attract many people to that area. That can be good for tourism, but _____ is happy if it creates a lot of traffic. Some people also get annoyed because public money has been spent on _____ that they don't actually like.

31 **Work in pairs.** Take turns tossing the cube. Use one of the words in a question. Your partner will answer, using the other word.

Go to p. 171.

> Do you have something to do this weekend?

> Well, I want to go to the movies, but I don't have anyone to go with.

When we write to give instructions or explain a process, it's important to explain each step clearly. To introduce each step, we use the following words or phrases:

first	second	then	next
after that	at the end	finally	

32 **Read the model.** How does the writer introduce each new step? Underline the words and phrases.

How to paint a mural in your area

Do you ever wish that you could make your neighborhood more exciting, more interesting, or just more beautiful? One simple way to change a place is to create a piece of public art. In this essay, I'm going to explain how you can paint a mural on a wall in your town or city.

First, you should decide what the subject of your mural will be. Think of something interesting that will have a positive effect on people. Second, choose your location. If you want people to see your mural, look for a place that a lot of people pass through each day. Then, of course, you'll need to get permission from the property owner and from your local town council, too.

Next, contact local neighborhood groups, schools, charities, and businesses. Ask them for ideas about what they want to see. They will be affected by this piece of art, so you want to get them on your side. If you're lucky, they might offer to give you materials, or even help you with the work.

After that, you need to make a plan for your painting. Sketch out your design, and decide what materials you'll need. Think about the colors and shapes you want to use.

Finally, paint your mural! When it's finished, invite people from your local community to view it. Take lots of photographs, and share this new piece of public art on social media.

33 **Work in pairs.** How many steps in the process does the writer mention? What are they?

34 **Write.** Imagine you are going to create a piece of public art in your school or community. Explain how you will create it.

NATIONAL GEOGRAPHIC

Learn from Art

"Hope is more powerful than fear. And to see that through visual arts is incredible."
—Shannon Galpin
National Geographic Adventurer and Humanitarian

1. **Watch scene 7.2.**

2. Find out about and visit public art in your area. Think about the meaning behind the art. What's the message? What does it teach you? Explain.

3. Think of a positive message that you would like to share with others. Then imagine how you could use art to communicate this message. Make a sketch of your idea, and explain it.

Make an Impact

A **Plan and make a presentation about public art.**

· Find out about a piece of public art that you like.

· Collect photos and information about the artist, the work, and its message.

· Make your presentation. Explain why you chose the piece.

B **Organize and hold an art show.**

· Invite your friends and classmates to share their own drawings, paintings, or sculptures. Collect at least five pieces.

· Write a description of each piece of artwork. Say who created it, when, and what it means.

· Display the art and information around the class. Answer your classmates' questions on the art.

C **Plan and write a biography of a local artist.**

· Choose an artist from your region. Find out about this person's life and work.

· Write a short biography of the artist. Include photos of this person's work.

· Present your biography to the class.

La mano en la arena (Hand in the Sand),
by Mario Irarrázabal, Punta del Este, Uruguay

Don't Panic!

"Fear is always there. You just need
to know how to manage it."
—Jimmy Chin

Photographer Jimmy Chin took this photo of a risk-taking climber in Yosemite National Park, California, USA.

1. Look at the photo. How does it make you feel? How do you think the person in the photo feels?

2. Can you control your fear? What do you do when you feel afraid? Explain, with examples.

3. When can it be good to feel fear? When can it be bad? Give examples.

1 **What types of natural disasters are there?**
What happens during each one? Discuss.
Then listen and read. TR: 93

In March 2015, a terrifying **wildfire** went through Cape Town, South Africa. "It was moving 65 km (40 mi.) in a single day and destroying everything in its path. We couldn't **breathe** because of the smoke, and we couldn't **escape**," said one Cape Town resident. Wildfires can start in forests or on open land, and the **flames** spread very quickly. Sometimes they start because the weather is hot and dry, but mostly humans cause wildfires. We can prevent them by **carefully** controlling

Other natural **disasters** are impos prevent. A hurricane—also called a t or a **cyclone**—is a rotating tropical st starts over the sea. When typhoon H **struck** the Philippines and Vietnam the winds reached over 100 kph (63 n caused massive destruction. Six thou people were killed, and more than tw had to leave their homes. Today we c accurately predict these storms, and attention to severe weather **warning**

Unlike a storm, an **earthquake** is usually completely unexpected. A huge earthquake hit Pakistan in October 2015. "The ground was **shaking**," said one Islamabad resident, who was at work at the time. "But worse than that was the sound of the earthquake. It was a horrible noise." Earthquakes usually don't last more than a minute, but their effects can be **terrible**. Buildings **collapse** and this can sometimes cause fires and floods. It can be very difficult to find **survivors** in the damaged areas.

These are just three examples of how powerful—and deadly—nature can be. But humans have the resources to handle these disasters. We can use technology to make predictions, take practical steps to make our environment safer, and work together when things go wrong.

A view of a wildfire from the inside of a car

2 **Learn new words.** Listen and repeat. TR: 94

3 **Work in pairs.** Discuss the three natural disasters described in the text. Which one would you be most afraid of? Why?

129

4 **Read and write the words from the list.** Make any necessary changes.

breathe	carefully	disaster	escape	shake
strike	survivor	terrible	warning	wildfire

_____ can happen anywhere and at any time. But for adventurers like National Geographic photographer Jimmy Chin, danger is part of daily life. Jimmy has to be ready to act when things go wrong. In 2008, Jimmy and two friends went on an expedition to Meru, one of the most difficult mountains to climb in the Himalayas. But although they prepared very _____ for the expedition, the weather was _____ . Just 100 m (328 ft.) from the top of the mountain, they had to turn back. In the same year, Jimmy nearly died after an avalanche _____ while he was skiing. Hundreds of tons of snow fell without _____ . The force of the snow covering his body made it difficult for him to _____ . Avalanches of this size rarely have _____ , and Jimmy was very lucky to _____ from the snow. Amazingly, just a few months later, Jimmy and his friends again attempted to climb Meru. This time they were successful!

Jimmy Chin

5 **Learn new words.** Listen for these words and match them to the definitions. Then listen and repeat. **TR: 95 and 96**

to pay attention to	to predict	to prevent	unexpected

1. _____ say that something will happen

2. _____ sudden and surprising

3. _____ notice or observe

4. _____ stop from happening

6 **Choose an activity.**

1. **Work independently.** Make a list of the natural disasters that threaten your area. Think about how to prepare for each one. Share your ideas with the class.

2. **Work in pairs.** Choose a natural disaster. Create a poster to educate people about what to do if this type of disaster strikes.

3. **Work in groups.** Find out about a recent natural disaster. Prepare a short presentation to tell your class what happened.

Telling a story	Showing interest
First of all, <u>there was this terrible noise outside</u>. The next thing I knew, <u>the ground started to shake</u>. Suddenly <u>all the books fell off of the bookshelves</u>.	Wow! I bet that was <u>scary</u>! So what happened then? No way! What did you do?

7 **Listen.** How do the speakers tell and show interest in the story? Write the words and phrases you hear. TR: 98

8 **Read and complete the dialogue.**

Emilia: Did I ever tell you about the earthquake last year?

Vicente: No, you didn't.

Emilia: Well, it was when we lived in Illapel in Chile. It was about 8 o'clock in the evening. _____ , I felt the ground start to move.

Vicente: No way! What _____ ?

Emilia: My mom and dad and I all got under the table. The walls were shaking, and then _____ all the lights went out.

Vicente: Wow! _____ scary!

Emilia: Yes, it was. Then _____ , a bookcase fell onto the floor right next to me.

Vicente: _____ then? Was everyone OK?

Emilia: The shaking continued for about three minutes, but everyone was OK.

9 **Work in pairs.** Toss a coin and move. (Heads = 1 space; tails = 2 spaces) Tell a story about the topic on the space. It can be real or invented. Your partner will listen and show interest. Then your partner must guess if your story is true.

> There was a cyclone in my grandparents' village last month. First of all, they heard the warning.

> So what happened then?

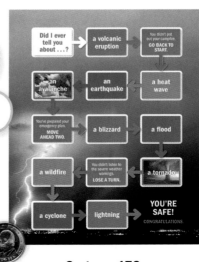

10 **Work in pairs.** Talk about an important event in your life. Your partner will show interest in your story. Then switch roles.

Go to p. 173.

131

GRAMMAR TR: 99

Simple past vs. past progressive: Talking about the past

What **did** the elephants **do** when they heard the noise? They **didn't make** a sound, but they **turned** around and **ran** away from the water.

Where **were** the birds **going**? They **weren't flying** north. They **were heading** south.

The day before the earthquake **struck**, all the animals in the nature reserve **were making** a lot of noise.

My cat **was trying** to hide when the storm **started**.

Ban's rescue

11 **Read.** Complete the paragraph with the simple-past or past-progressive forms of the verbs in parentheses.

In March 2011, a terrible tsunami _____ (strike) Japan. Many people _____ (die), and many more houses were destroyed. Three weeks after the tsunami, a rescue team _____ (look for) survivors in the sea. Suddenly they _____ (notice) the roof of a house. It _____ (float) on the water. A small brown dog _____ (sit) on the roof. The team _____ (save) the dog and _____ (bring) it back to shore. But they _____ (can't) find the dog's owner. Just a few days later, the dog's owner _____ (watch) TV when a news report about the dog came on. "I _____ (see) the rescue on the news, and I _____ (know) it was my dog, Ban!" she said. Now Ban and her owner are together again.

12 **Work independently.** Listen to the information about animal behavior before the Indian Ocean tsunami of December 2004. Then write questions about the story. TR: 100

1. What /animals / do / before the tsunami? _____
2. What / people / at the park / watch? _____
3. What / the elephants / do? _____
4. Where / the flamingos / fly? _____
5. What / the buffalo / do? _____
6. Where / they / run? _____

13 **Work in pairs.** Listen again. Then take turns asking and answering the questions from Activity 12. TR: 101

> What were the animals doing before the tsunami?

> They were acting strangely.

14 **Learn new words.** Listen to learn about a time when dolphins helped people. Then listen and repeat. TR: 102 and 103

There are many stories about brave dolphins who have tried to help humans when they **are in trouble**. In October 2004, a group of dolphins started to swim around four swimmers. The dolphins knew that a shark was **chasing** the swimmers, so the dolphins formed a circle to protect the group. The people didn't know what was **happening** at first, but the dolphins stayed with the people until they were safely back on land.

15 **Work in pairs.** Listen to the story again. Then use the prompts below to summarize the story. TR: 104

1. four people / go for a swim

   Four people went for a swim.
   _____

2. the swimmers / notice a group of dolphins

   _____

3. the dolphins / make a circle

   _____

4. a great white shark / chase

   _____

5. brave dolphins / keep the shark away

   _____

16 **Work in groups.** Think about a time when you were in trouble and someone helped you. Use the words in the box to tell your story.

be in trouble	brave	chase	happen	prevent	scared	terrible

17 **Before you read, discuss in pairs.** Based on the title and the photo, what do you think the reading is about?

18 **Learn new words.** Find these words in the text. Can you think of a synonym for each word? Use a thesaurus to help. Then listen and repeat. TR: 105

eventually	to scream
to sense	terrified

19 **While you read, try to visualize, or see a picture of in your mind, the events Jimmy describes.** TR: 106

20 **After you read, work in pairs to answer these questions.**

1. Which sport has Jimmy been doing longer—climbing or skiing?
2. What were Jeremy and Xavier doing while Jimmy was skiing down the mountain?
3. Why did Jimmy turn around to see the avalanche?
4. What images does Jimmy use to show the power and the weight of the snow?
5. How did Xavier and Jeremy feel when they found Jimmy alive at the bottom of the valley?
6. What does Jimmy think is important in life?

21 **Work in pairs.** Draw four very simple pictures to show what happened to Jimmy.

THE POWER OF SNOW

Jimmy Chin recalls the day he was thrown more than 600 m (2,000 ft.) in an avalanche—and survived!

An avalanche

From a young age, I've had a really deep connection with being outside. I've been skiing since I was eight or nine years old, and I've been climbing since I was in college.

I've been on expeditions in China, Pakistan, Nepal, India, Tanzania, Chad, Mali, South Africa, Borneo, and Argentina, among other places. But it was in my home country, the USA, that I came closest to death.

It was April 1, 2011. I was filming and skiing in the Tetons, a mountain range in Wyoming. I was with my friends Jeremy Jones and Xavier de la Rue, both experienced snowboarders. That day, we had finished going down a steep, narrow track, called "The Sliver," and we were descending another peak. I was the last person to ski. Jeremy and Xavier were watching me from a safe area. Suddenly, I heard someone scream. I turned around and saw the whole mountain start to move behind me. It was a massive avalanche. The kind of avalanche that destroys trees, cars, buses, even houses. Tens of thousands of tons of snow were coming straight down the mountain behind me. I felt the snow push me forward, hundreds of meters, and then cover me. It was so heavy that I couldn't breathe. And then it pushed me forward again and up, out of the snowpack. I looked around, and for a few seconds I actually stopped being terrified. I had a moment to pause and to look at the power of the avalanche. Imagine snow, the same weight as a thousand airplanes, falling like an ocean all around you. You don't ever sense that kind of power.

I looked down into the bottom of the valley. I could see trees that were 30 m (98 ft.) tall, but they looked tiny to me because I was so far away. "OK, I'm going all the way to the bottom!" I thought. Then the snow pushed me again down the mountain another 450 m (1,500 ft.). I thought the force of the snow would destroy me, it was so powerful. But eventually, I felt the avalanche slow down and I just popped right out of the snow at the bottom of the valley.

It took Jeremy and Xavier about twenty minutes to reach me. There was a pile of debris across the bottom of the mountain 300 m (1,000 ft.) wide. They were certain that I was dead. They couldn't believe it when they saw me. I was so lucky.

Has the experience changed me? Do I think about life differently? I don't know, maybe. But I do know that it's important to live your life with meaning. Life is a gift, so use it wisely.

22 Discuss in groups.

1. What is the scariest experience that you have ever had? How did it change you?

2. Should people practice dangerous sports? Why or why not? What are they risking for themselves? What effect might it have on others?

3. Make a list of five very dangerous sports and activities, and put them in order from most to least dangerous. Explain your order.

23 **Before you watch, discuss in pairs.** Look at the photo. What do you see? How does it make you feel? What do you think this person experienced?

A cast of human remains uncovered at the Pompeii site

24 **Work in pairs.** You're going to watch a video called *A Day in Pompeii*. Predict what the video will be about. Where is Pompeii? What famous natural disaster happened there?

25 **Watch scene 8.1. While you watch, check your answers from Activity 24.** Were they correct? What did you already know about Pompeii?

26 **After you watch, work in pairs to answer the questions.**

1. Why did Pliny's uncle take his boat to Pompeii?
2. Why didn't Pliny go with his uncle?
3. What could Pliny see the next morning?
4. What happened to Pliny's uncle?
5. How many people lived in Pompeii in 79 CE? How many people live in this area today?
6. According to experts, how often do these kinds of eruptions happen?

27 **Work in pairs.** In the final line of the video, the narrator says, "The next one is overdue." What does she mean? Why do you think people still live in the area around Mt. Vesuvius? Would you want to live there? Why or why not?

28 **Work in pairs.** Look again at the photo. With your partner, invent the story of this person's life. Tell what he/she was doing when the volcano erupted. Share your story with the class.

29 **Choose an activity.**

1. **Work independently.** Find out about another famous volcanic eruption. Write a paragraph to describe what happened.

2. **Work in pairs.** Role-play an interview between Pliny the Younger and a reporter who wants to know what happened at Pompeii.

3. **Work in groups.** Imagine that you were living near Pompeii on the day of the eruption. Write a journal entry about what happened.

GRAMMAR TR: 107

Present perfect vs. present perfect progressive: Expressing the duration of activities

The fire **has burned** 300 km² (186 sq. mi.) since October 3.

He **has fought** many fires in his career as a firefighter.

He**'s been** a firefighter for ten years.

He **has** always **loved** his job.

The fire **has been burning** since three o'clock this morning.

He**'s been fighting** this fire for several hours.

---

30 **Listen to the news report.** Then use the correct form of the verbs to complete the article below. TR: 108

| already destroy | live | move | pack up | prepare | spread | work |

The fire in Lake County, which was first reported on October 15, _____ over the last ten days. It _____ more than 250 km² (155 sq. mi.) of forest. Firefighters _____ all day and all night, but the fire _____ quickly toward Middletown. Many Middletown residents _____ to leave the town throughout the day. They _____ their most important possessions. It's a sad day for them, many of whom _____ in Middletown for many years.

31 **Work independently.** Write true sentences about yourself and your experiences.

1. for three years

_____

2. since January

_____

3. since this morning

_____

32 **Work in pairs.** Pick a card. Ask a question, using the phrase on your card. Answer your partner's questions.

How long have you liked your favorite band?

I've liked my favorite band for about a year. And you?

Go to p. 175.

like / favorite band

WRITING

When we write a narrative essay, we tell a story. In the final paragraph, we need to say why the story is important. This concluding paragraph should explain the message of the story.

33 **Read the model.** Work in pairs to identify the message of the story.

Aron Ralston is a very experienced climber and hiker. He has been climbing, skiing, and hiking since he was a young boy. But even experienced climbers can make mistakes. The mistake Aron made on April 26, 2003, nearly cost him his life.

Aron was hiking through the Utah's Bluejohn Canyon when he fell down a narrow canyon. His right arm got trapped behind a rock. He tried to escape, but the rock was too big and too heavy. Aron was stuck in the canyon for five and a half days. He was hungry, thirsty, and very tired. He wanted to cut off his arm because that was the only way to escape. On his sixth day in the canyon, he managed to break his arm and then cut it off with the small knife he had. He hiked out of the canyon and finally saw other people. They called the emergency services, and a helicopter took him to the hospital.

Aron Ralston

Aron lost his arm, but he's happy to be alive. He still climbs and hikes regularly. He knows that he made a mistake when he didn't tell anyone about his plans. His bravery helped him survive this terrible accident. Now he makes sure he tells others when he's going on an adventure. He also gives talks around the world about his experience to help others learn from his mistake.

34 **Work in pairs.** What would you do in Aron's situation?

35 **Write.** Write a true story about survival. It could be about yourself, someone you know, or a famous person. Write a strong concluding paragraph.

Be Prepared

"Don't put yourself into dangerous situations where risks are high, your level of control is low, and you aren't prepared."
—Jimmy Chin

National Geographic Explorer, Climber/Photographer

1. Watch scene 8.2.

2. Think of a dangerous situation that you've experienced. Were you prepared? Were you in control? Explain.

3. Think of an adventure you'd like to experience. Would it be dangerous? What risks are there? What should you do to prepare? Name three things.

Make an Impact

A **Write and perform a skit.**

· Choose a natural disaster, and find out the best ways to handle it.

· Write a dialogue between a safety worker and a person that he/she is helping to prevent, prepare for, or react to the disaster.

· Perform your skit for the class.

B **Create a comic strip.**

· Find out about an explorer or adventurer who survived in a dangerous situation.

· Think about the key events in his/her story.

· Create a comic strip to tell the story.

C **Write a news article.**

· Go online to read about animals that have helped to save human lives.

· Choose your favorite story. Continue researching to learn more about what happened.

· Write a newspaper article summarizing the story. Include a photo in your article.

Express Yourself

1 **Read and listen to the information about a public art project.** TR: 109

WHAT ARE YOU WAITING FOR?

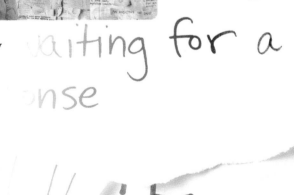

A teen installs a poster on the construction fence, 2013. Photograph by Filip Wolak

In 2013, participants in the Whitney Museum's teen program worked together with artist Gary Simmons to create a new piece of public art. As they were trying to think of a theme for the project, many of the young people spoke about how much time they spend waiting . . . for friends, for trains, for phone calls, to become adults. They decided to base their public art project around this idea.

The teens talked to their peers and friends and collected responses to the question: *What are you waiting for?*

Then they all worked together to create a collage of these responses. The collage was photographed and made into a series of large posters. The posters were displayed at the construction site for the new Whitney Museum building in New York City.

These are some of the responses to the question *What are you waiting for?*

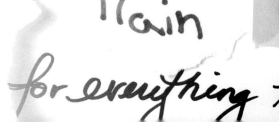

I am waiting for an email

A good thing come my w...

...od time
...uch the
...world.

DIENCE OF ONE

–I am wait...
day when "so...
is not separa...

What Are You Waiting For? poster detail,
2013. Photograph by Sarah Anne Ward

$w@g

A
chance

PROVE
YSELF

I'm
son...
m...

...DS & BEACHES
...NIGHT-STAND...
...MMER DAYS
...NDS & WINE & N...
...AVELS & SUITC...
... & ADVENTURES
...NETY & PICNICS &
ICHES & BEDS & CHOCOLATE & HIGH·HE...
DECISIONS & GOOD DECISIONS & LO...
MS & MUSICAL THEATRE & AAPPY...
EAM & FLOOR·LENGTH DRESSES...
VEL & RE·RUNS & MAKING...
BUT SURELY & LOVE

waitin...
first c...

2 Work in groups.

1. Would you like to take part in a public art project like this? Why or why not?

2. Imagine that you're creating a similar piece of public art. Individually, ask classmates to complete the following sentence: *Always be prepared for . . .* Then discuss classmates' responses in your groups.

3 Connect ideas. In Unit 7, you learned about public art. In Unit 8, you learned about risks and dangerous situations. How are these topics connected? How can we use art to express our feelings and fears?

4 Choose an activity.

1. Choose a topic:
   • public art
   • danger

2. Choose a way to express yourself:
   • a poem
   • a video blog
   • a piece of public art

3. Present your work.

Unit 1

Schwa (/ə/) sound

1 **Listen.** Notice the pronunciation of the vowels in the underlined syllables. TR: 110

vege-<u>ta</u>-<u>ble</u>   **pur**-<u>ple</u>   re-<u>pre</u>-**sent**

Vowels in unstressed syllables often have the schwa sound. Schwa is a relaxed /uh/ sound. The symbol in dictionaries looks like an upside-down e (/ə/).

Many common suffixes, or word endings, are unstressed.

ner-<u>vous</u>   **na**-<u>tion</u>

Unstressed suffixes often have the schwa sound. The schwa is the most common sound in the English language.

2 **Listen and repeat.** Circle the unstressed syllables with a schwa sound. TR: 111

pop-u-**la**-tion	**dan**-ge-rous	con-**nec**-tions
ex-**am**-ple	sit-u-**a**-tions	**hos**-pi-tals
de-**li**-cious	at-**ten**-tion	tra-**di**-tion-al

3 **Work in pairs.** Complete the sentences with words from Activity 2. Then listen and check. Take turns saying the sentences correctly. TR: 112

1. People have ____connections____ with colors. For _____ , green makes people feel calm.

2. A _____ color for weddings is white.

3. About five percent of the _____ is colorblind.

4. Walls in _____ are not usually painted black or other dark colors.

5. People pay _____ when they see the color yellow. It's used on traffic signs to warn people of _____ _____ .

Unit 2

Pronunciation of *-s* endings

1 **Listen.** Notice the different pronunciations for each *-s* ending. TR: 113

The *-s* ending has three possible pronunciations. It sounds like:

• *iz* when the final sound of a verb has a s, z, x, sh, ch, or j sound. These sounds add another syllable to the word.

• *s* when the final sound is *f, k, p,* or *t*.

• *z* when the final sound is a vowel or any other consonant.

iz	*s*	*z*
wash<u>es</u>	sleep<u>s</u>	say<u>s</u>
rais<u>es</u>	look<u>s</u>	give<u>s</u>
danc<u>es</u>	help<u>s</u>	read<u>s</u>

2 **Listen and repeat.** Listen again and write the word you hear in the space. TR: 114

1. Jill ____sleeps____ regularly. She _____ to bed early.

2. Lack of sleep _____ your mind. Your body _____ cells to combat illness as you sleep.

3. Jack usually _____ up late. He rarely _____ enough sleep because he _____ TV late at night.

3 **Work in pairs.** Write each verb from Activity 2 in the correct column. Listen to the completed chart to check your answers. TR: 115

iz as in *teaches*	*s* as in *talks*	*z* as in *says*
	sleeps	

Unit 3

Have to

1 **Listen.** Notice the pronunciation of *has to/have to* + verb. TR: 116

She <u>has to do</u> some research online.
They <u>have to be</u> careful.

The word *has* ends with a *z* sound, and *have* with a *v*, but when they are followed by *to* to suggest obligation, the final sounds usually change. They sound like *hasta* or *hafta*.

Gotta (the relaxed form of *got to*) is sometimes used informally after the short forms *'ve* (have) or *'s* (has). It sounds like *godda*.

You<u>'ve *gotta*</u> try this new site.
She<u>'s *gotta*</u> get a new computer.

2 **Listen and repeat.** Then complete the sentences. TR: 117

1. You _____ have to _____ be careful online.
2. He _____ get a new phone.
3. I _____ go offline now.
4. She _____ be more polite.
5. We _____ remember so many passwords. There _____ be an easier way to access our accounts.

3 **Work in pairs.** Take turns discussing the situations. Use *have to* or *gotta*.

> You have to tell your friend to be respectful.

1. Your friend is mean online. (*has to*)
2. An unfamiliar person keeps contacting you. (*gotta*)
3. Your mother wants to be your friend on a social-media site. (*gotta*)
4. You're constantly using your smartphone. (*have to*)

Unit 4

Verb *use* vs. *used to* + verb

1 **Listen.** Notice how *use* is pronounced when it's a main verb and when it's in the modal phrase *used to*. TR: 118

They didn't <u>use to</u> have many tools.
Researchers today <u>use</u> high-tech tools.
I <u>used to</u> see whales in the winter.
I <u>used</u> binoculars to get a closer look.

When *use* is a main verb, the *s* sounds like *z*. When it's in the modal phrase *used to*, it's pronounced like an *s* and sounds like *usta*.

2 **Listen and repeat.** Circle the pronunciation of the letter *s* in *use/used to*. TR: 119

1. He used to live near the ocean. (s) z
2. His family used their neighbor's boat. s z
3. We didn't use to swim much. s z
4. I used to collect small sea creatures. s z
5. I would use a jar to collect sand. s z
6. I used two of your tanks for the dive. s z

3 **Work in pairs.** Make sentences with *used to* and any of the phrases that were true about you in the past, but aren't true now.

> I used to swim in the ocean every day. I didn't use to play soccer.

swim in the ocean   play (a sport)

watch (TV show)   play (an instrument)

eat (food)   love (class)

walk to school   (your choice)

Unit 5

Linking

1 **Listen.** Notice how the words sound when said apart and together. **TR: 120**

can, even: They can even
I, am: I am   you, are: you are

Consonant sound to vowel sound: the consonant sound moves to the next word

can even = ca-neven

Vowel sound to vowel sound: a *y* or *w* sound is inserted. A *y* sound is inserted after *e*, *a*, and *i* sounds.

we are, they are, I am
  y   y   y

A *w* is inserted after *o* and *u* sounds.

no air, you are
 w   w

2 **Listen and repeat.** Listen again and write a *y* or a *w* under the appropriate links. **TR: 121**

1. This is the most beautiful place I've ever seen.

2. Some animals live where there is no oxygen.

3. I am fascinated by extremophiles.

3 **Work in pairs.** Listen and complete the dialogue. Then practice with your partner. **TR: 122**

A: Let's choose an _____ as a mascot for our team.

B: A tiger, maybe? Or an _____ ?

A: Let's think of a new _____ . Maybe a parasite?

B: No! That's a terrible idea! Why don't we _____ the team?

Unit 6

Going to, want to

1 **Listen.** Notice the pronunciation of *going to*. **TR: 123**

We're <u>going to</u> a restaurant.
We're <u>going to</u> eat late today.

When *going* is a main verb before the preposition *to*, the pronunciation is not relaxed.

When it's used to express the future, *going to* is often pronounced *gonna*.

Similarly, when *want to* is used before a main verb, it's often relaxed. It's pronounced *wanna*.

I don't <u>wanna</u> eat salad.

2 **Listen and repeat.** Write *going to* or *want to*. You will hear the reduced form. **TR: 124**

1. I _____ help students change their behavior so they don't throw away so much food. Joe is _____ help me organize my campaign. Do you _____ help, too?

2. Are we _____ have leftovers for dinner again? I don't _____ eat any more spaghetti!

3 **Work in pairs.** Listen to and repeat the questions. Then take turns asking and answering them. **TR: 125**

What are you gonna eat for breakfast tomorrow?

I don't know. I wanna eat something different. Maybe oatmeal with fruit.

1. What are you going to eat for breakfast tomorrow?
2. What exotic food would you want to try?
3. What do you want to do after high school?
4. Are you going to finish all your homework this week?

Unit 7

Word stress with suffixes

1 **Listen.** Notice the stress when the word forms change. TR: 126

base word	no change	syl. before
create	cre*ative*	crea*tiv*i*ty*
happy	**hap**pi*ness*	
organize	**or**gani*zer*	organi*za*tion
photo	**pho**to*graph*	photo**graph***ic*
pleasure	**plea**sur*able*	

The stress patterns of words with the same suffixes are usually the same.

- These suffixes do not change stress of the base word: *-ness, -er/-or, -graph, -able.*

- These suffixes have stress before the suffix: *-ity, -ic/-ical, -tion/-sion.*

2 **Listen and repeat.** Circle the stressed syllable in each group. TR: 127

1. pho-to-**gra**-phic
2. ex-hi-bi-tion
3. ex-hi-bi-tor
4. cre-a-tion
5. ar-tis-tic

6. em-ploy-er
7. i-ma-gi-na-tion
8. a-ware-ness
9. ad-ven-tur-er
10. per-mis-sion

3 **Work in pairs.** Listen and repeat. Then practice the conversation. TR: 128

A: We're going to an exhi**bi**tion. Do you want to come? The **ar**tist is very cre**a**tive.

B: Sure! Is the **ar**tist a **pain**ter?

A: No, she's a **sculp**tor. Her work aims to bring a**ware**ness to the environment.

B: Oh, I follow an organi**za**tion on social media that does that.

Unit 8

Sentence stress

1 **Listen.** Notice the strong and weak beats in the sentences. TR: 129

I have **ne**ver **seen** a tor**na**do.
He has sur**vived** an **a**valanche.
Did you **see** the **fire**?
Where did you **see** the **spi**der?

The words that carry more meaning in a sentence are pronounced more fully than other words. These words include nouns, verbs, adjectives, adverbs, question words (*who*), and negative forms (*didn't, never, not*).

Words that provide grammatical information are usually shortened or said quickly. These words include articles (*the, a, an*); pronouns (*he, she*); prepositions (*in, on*); and affirmative modals and other auxiliaries (*should, will, be, have, do*).

2 **Listen and repeat.** Underline the stressed words. Listen again and check your answers. Circle the stressed syllable in the words you underlined. TR: 130

1. Have you **ever gone skiing**?
2. Do you like scary movies?
3. Have you experienced an earthquake?
4. Which kind of natural disaster are you most afraid of?
5. What is the scariest animal you've seen?

3 **Work in pairs.** Ask and answer the questions in Activity 2. Give details.

Have you ever gone skiing?

Yes, I have. I've been skiing many times. I love it!

Irregular Verbs

Infinitive	Simple past	Past participle	Infinitive	Simple past	Past participle
be	were	been	leave	left	left
beat	beat	beaten	lend	lent	lent
become	became	become	let	let	let
begin	began	begun	lie (down)	lay	lain
bend	bent	bent	light	lit	lit
bet	bet	bet	lose	lost	lost
bite	bit	bitten	make	made	made
bleed	bled	bled	mean	meant	meant
blow	blew	blown	meet	met	met
break	broke	broken	overcome	overcame	overcome
bring	brought	brought	pay	paid	paid
build	built	built	put	put	put
burn	burned/burnt	burned/burnt	quit	quit	quit
buy	bought	bought	read	read	read
carry	carried	carried	ride	rode	ridden
catch	caught	caught	ring	rang	rung
choose	chose	chosen	rise	rose	risen
come	came	come	run	ran	run
cost	cost	cost	say	said	said
cut	cut	cut	see	saw	seen
deal	dealt	dealt	sell	sold	sold
dig	dug	dug	send	sent	sent
dive	dove/dived	dived	set	set	set
do	did	done	sew	sewed	sewn
draw	drew	drawn	shake	shook	shaken
drink	drank	drunk	shine	shone	shone
drive	drove	driven	show	showed	shown
dry	dried	dried	shrink	shrank	shrunk
eat	ate	eaten	shut	shut	shut
fall	fell	fallen	sing	sang	sung
feed	fed	fed	sink	sank	sunk
feel	felt	felt	sit	sat	sat
fight	fought	fought	sleep	slept	slept
find	found	found	slide	slid	slid
flee	fled	fled	speak	spoke	spoken
fly	flew	flown	spend	spent	spent
forbid	forbade	forbidden	spin	spun	spun
forget	forgot	forgotten	stand	stood	stood
forgive	forgave	forgiven	steal	stole	stolen
freeze	froze	frozen	stick	stuck	stuck
fry	fried	fried	sting	stung	stung
get	got	gotten	stink	stank	stunk
give	gave	given	strike	struck	struck/stricken
go	went	gone	swear	swore	sworn
grind	ground	ground	sweep	swept	swept
grow	grew	grown	swim	swam	swum
hang	hung	hung	swing	swung	swung
have	had	had	take	took	taken
hear	heard	heard	teach	taught	taught
hide	hid	hidden	tear	tore	torn
hit	hit	hit	tell	told	told
hold	held	held	think	thought	thought
hurt	hurt	hurt	throw	threw	thrown
keep	kept	kept	understand	understood	understood
kneel	knelt/kneeled	knelt/kneeled	wake	woke	woken
knit	knitted/knit	knitted/knit	wear	wore	worn
know	knew	known	weave	wove/weaved	woven/weaved
lay	laid	laid	win	won	won
lead	led	led	write	wrote	written

Making a presentation

1 **Listen and read.** TR: 131

Adam: Good morning, class. Today, we'd like to talk to you about technology.

Amalia: The focus of our presentation is smartphones. We'll begin by listing the different uses of smartphones.

Adam: The next thing we'd like to talk about is how often teens use smartphones. Please look at this chart. Notice that most teens use their smartphones for over four hours a day.

[...]

Adam: In conclusion, smartphones can be both helpful and harmful. Does anybody have any questions or comments?

Beginning	Middle	End
• Good morning/afternoon, class. • Today, I'd/we'd like to talk to you about . . . • The focus of my/our presentation is . . . • I'll/We'll begin by . . .	• The next thing I'd /we'd like to talk about is . . . • Please look at . . . • Notice that . . . • Moving right along, . . . • Any questions?	• In conclusion, . . . • And so, . . . • Does anybody have any questions or comments?

Asking for and giving information

2 **Listen and read.** TR: 132

Julia: Hey, Carlos. Could you tell me what the math homework is?

Carlos: As far as I know, we just need to study for the test.

Julia: I wonder what's on it. Do you have any idea?

Carlos: Well, I heard that it's all of Unit 10 and the first part of Unit 11.

Julia: Thanks!

Carlos: Sure. I'd like to know if we'll be able to use our calculators.

Julia: I don't know.

Asking for information	Responding
• Can/Could you tell me . . . ? • I'd like to know . . . • I wonder . . . • Do you know? • Do you have any idea?	• I've heard/read that . . . • As far as I know, . . . • I'm not sure, but I think . . . • I'd say . . . • I don't know.

Interrupting

3 **Listen and read.** TR: 133

Mr. Silva: Alberto Santos-Dumont wasn't just a flight pioneer. He also helped make wristwatches popular among men! Using a pocket watch was not practical on a plane, so he asked his friend Louis Cartier for help.

Renato: Excuse me, Mr. Silva. Can I ask a question? Could you spell the last name?

Mr. Silva: Of course. It's C-A-R-T-I-E-R. OK. Back to the story. Cartier then built the first pilot wristwatch! Santos-Dumont wore it . . .

Renato: Sorry to interrupt, but how did Santos-Dumont help make wristwatches popular?

Mr. Silva: Great question, Renato! Santos-Dumont was a very popular person. People started noticing his watch and asking about it.

Interrupting	Interrupting to ask a question or add information	Interrupting someone who interrupted you
• Excuse me. • Sorry to interrupt. • Sorry, but . . .	• Can I ask a question? • May I say/ask something? • I'd like to say something. • Can I add something? • I'd like to comment on that.	• OK. Back to . . . • I have something I'd like to add. • Can I continue?

Agreeing and disagreeing

4 **Listen and read.** TR: 134

Lin: I think we should do a video for our project.

Chang: I agree.

Mei: No way! Not again. We did a video last time. Why don't we do an online presentation?

Lin: I'm not so sure. Presentations can be boring.

Chang: Actually, I think it's a great idea. Presentations don't have to be boring. We can add music and sound effects! Maybe we can do a bit of both. We can do a short video and include it in the presentation.

Lin: I guess so!

Mei: Exactly! A presentation *and* a video!

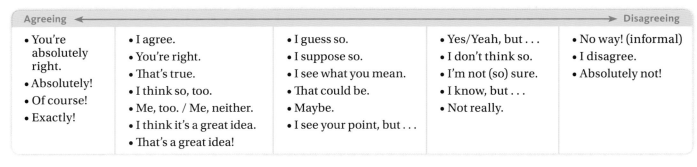

Agreeing				Disagreeing
• You're absolutely right. • Absolutely! • Of course! • Exactly!	• I agree. • You're right. • That's true. • I think so, too. • Me, too. / Me, neither. • I think it's a great idea. • That's a great idea!	• I guess so. • I suppose so. • I see what you mean. • That could be. • Maybe. • I see your point, but . . .	• Yes/Yeah, but . . . • I don't think so. • I'm not (so) sure. • I know, but . . . • Not really.	• No way! (informal) • I disagree. • Absolutely not!

Making and receiving phone calls

5 **Listen and read.** TR: 135

Mr. Alonso:	Hello.
Juan:	Hi, Mr. Alonso. It's Juan. Is Beto there?
Mr. Alonso:	Hi, Juan. Yes, he is. I'll get him for you.
Juan:	Thanks!
Mr. Alonso:	Hello?
Juan:	Hi, Mr. Alonso. It's Juan. May I speak with Beto, please?
Mr. Alonso:	Hi, Juan. I'm sorry, but he's busy right now. Can I have him call you back?
Juan:	That would be great. Thank you!
Mr. Alonso:	Good bye, Juan.

Greetings		Asking to speak to someone	Responding		
• Hello. • Hi, (Mr. Alonso).	• It's (Juan).	• Is (Beto) there? • May I speak with (Beto), please? • Can I talk to (Beto)?	• I'll get (him) for you.		• Thanks.
			• (He) isn't here. • I'm sorry. (He's) not home. • (He's) busy right now.	• Can I have (him) call you back? • Would you like to leave a message?	• That would be great. • No, thanks. I'll call back later.

Apologizing

6 **Listen and read.** TR: 136

Natalie:	Did you send Aunt Anna a birthday card?
Juan:	Oops. I forgot it was her birthday.
Natalie:	I didn't either. I'm terrible with dates.
Juan:	I can't believe I forgot it. I'm usually good at remembering birthdays.
Natalie:	Oh! My mistake. Her birthday is next Friday.
Juan:	That's a relief!
Natalie:	Sorry!

Apologizing	
• Sorry. • I'm sorry. • Excuse me. • Oops.	• My fault / mistake. • I can't believe I did / said that. • I'm terrible with dates / names.

Responding to news

7 **Listen and read.** TR: 137

Good news

Fatima:	I have some good news to tell you.
Adil:	Really? What is it?
Fatima:	Those paintings that we entered in the upcoming art show were accepted!
Adil:	That's great news!
Fatima:	I know. The show is next week. Well done!
Adil:	Wow! That's fantastic!
Fatima:	I know. I can't wait.
Adil:	Congratulations! I can't wait to see your work.
Fatima:	Thank you! I can't wait for the show.

Good news

- Congratulations!
- That's fantastic!
- I'm so happy for you.
- That's great news!
- Well done!
- Good / Great job!
- Lucky you!

8 **Listen and read.** TR: 138

Bad news

Fatima:	Uh-oh.
Adil:	What is it?
Fatima:	I have some bad news to tell you. I'm sorry to tell you this, but your painting didn't make it into the art show.
Adil:	Oh no! What happened?
Fatima:	Your entry arrived late.
Adil:	Oh no, that stinks.
Fatima:	I know. I'm so sorry.
Adil:	Oh well. That's too bad. Next time I'll make sure to send it ahead of time.
Fatima:	If there's anything I can do, let me know.

Bad news

- Oh no!
- How terrible / sad / awful!
- I'm so sorry to tell you / hear that.
- That must have been awful / terrible.
- That's horrible/ too bad / awful.
- That stinks.

Begin by saying:

Polar bears have white fur.

Correct by saying:

Cats can see color. They just don't see as many different shades as humans do.

Begin by saying:

Flamingos are pink.

Correct by saying:

The Golden Gate Bridge isn't red. It's a special shade of orange called "international orange."

Begin by saying:

The Golden Gate Bridge is red.

Correct by saying:

There are no colors in black light. Black is the color you see when there is no light. White is the color you see when blue, red, and yellow light are mixed together.

Begin by saying:

Cats can only see in black and white.

Correct by saying:

Bulls are colorblind! They get angry when people move suddenly or fast.

Begin by saying:

Bulls get angry when they see the color red.

Correct by saying:

Flamingos aren't pink. They're gray. They get their pink color from eating a lot of pink shrimp.

Begin by saying:

Black light is made from a lot of different colors all mixed together.

Correct by saying:

A polar bear's fur isn't white. It's clear. It reflects the light, and this makes it look white.

Start

It's _____ brightest color in the store.

What colors are _____ books in your bag?

She is _____ only girl in our family.

_____ moon is very bright tonight.

I want to buy _____ new computer.

DANGER!

Lose a turn.

I had _____ apple for breakfast.

GOOD LUCK!

Move forward 2 spaces.

She's _____ most intelligent girl in our class.

BAD LUCK!

Move back 6 spaces.

Are you _____ student at this school?

_____ color blue is very popular around the world.

Many restaurants use _____ color red.

Is that _____ plane in the sky?

I love swimming in _____ sea.

BAD LUCK!

Move back 2 spaces.

He lives in _____ small house in Buenos Aires.

My cat is _____ cat sitting on the rug.

Finish

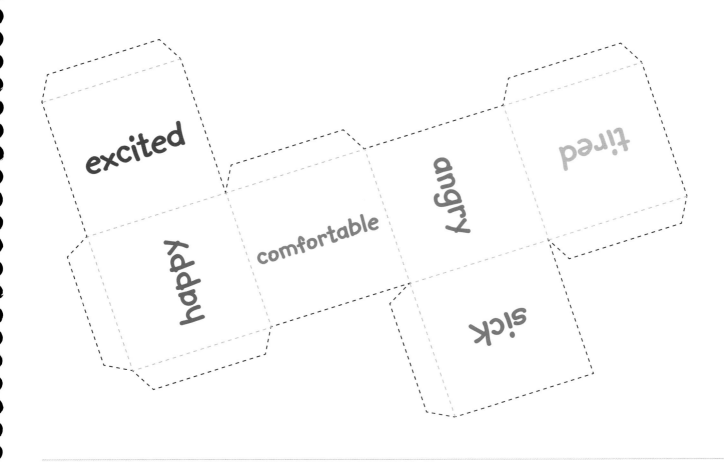

Unit 3 Cutouts Use with Activity 9 on p. 47.

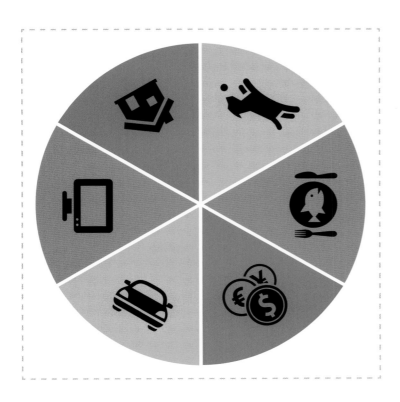

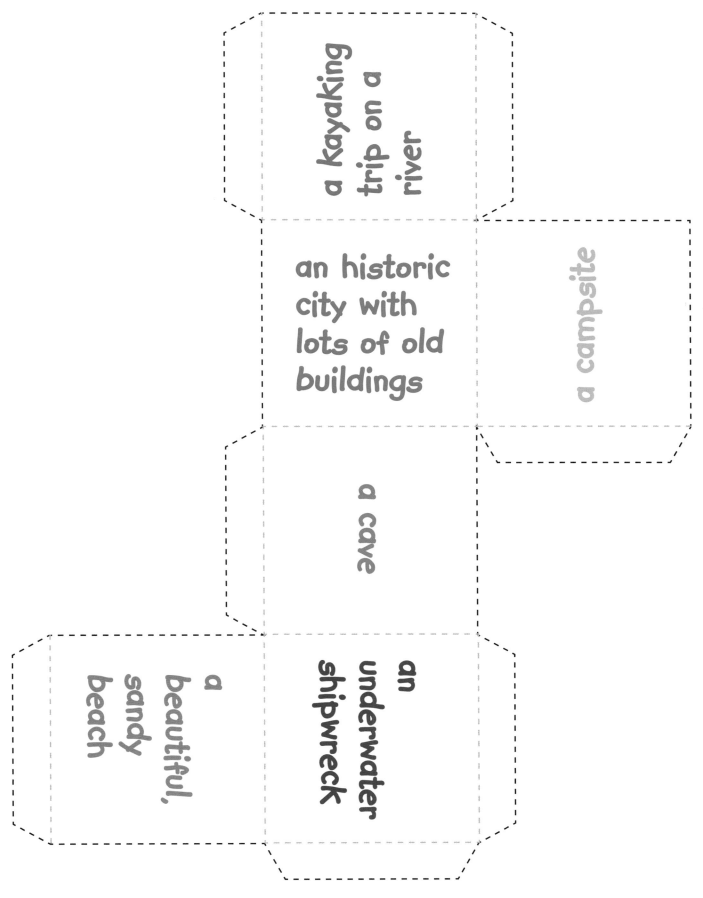

a kayaking trip on a river

an historic city with lots of old buildings

a campsite

a cave

a beautiful, sandy beach

an underwater shipwreck

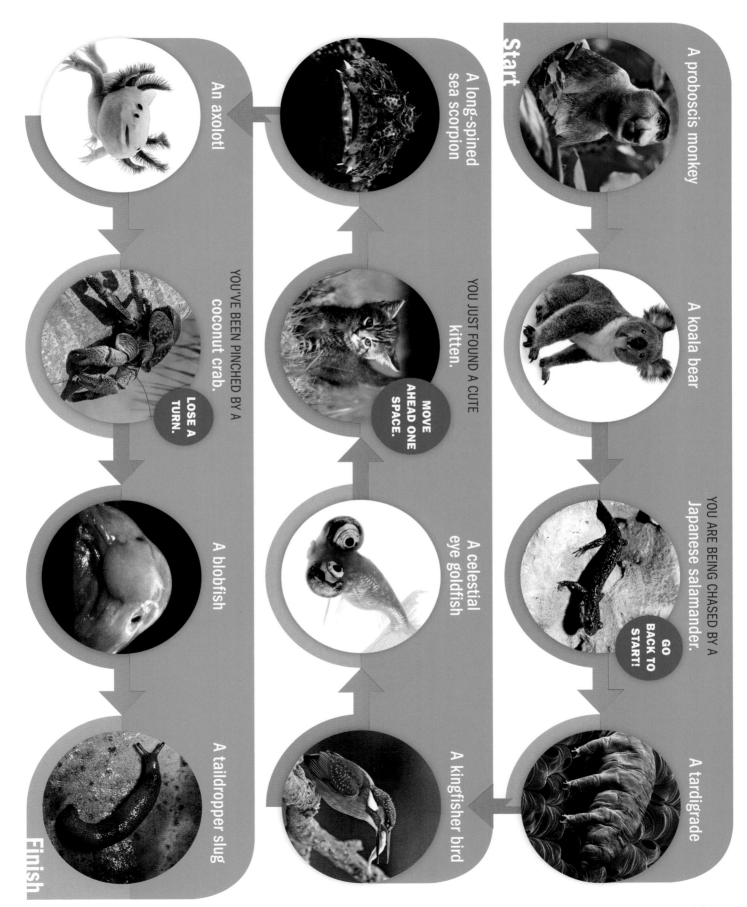

Start

A proboscis monkey

A long-spined sea scorpion

An axolotl

A koala bear

YOU JUST FOUND A CUTE kitten.

MOVE AHEAD ONE SPACE.

YOU'VE BEEN PINCHED BY A coconut crab.

LOSE A TURN.

YOU ARE BEING CHASED BY A Japanese salamander.

GO BACK TO START!

A celestial eye goldfish

A blobfish

A tardigrade

A kingfisher bird

A taildropper slug

Finish

Category	Me	People similar to me
Number of people in the family		
Height		
Distance between home and school		
Wake-up time		
Bedtime		
Your choice: _____		

Each year, 1.3 billion tons of edible food is wasted worldwide.

If we reduce our waste, we could produce enough food to feed everyone in the world.

The amount of food wasted in the European Union each year is enough to go around the world one time.

Twenty-eight percent of the world's farmland is used to make food that doesn't get eaten.

Consumers are starting to change their habits. Ugly food campaigns are becoming popular.

One billion people in the world are hungry. That's one in seven people!

Food waste costs $750 billion each year, and this doesn't include meat and seafood.

Tristram Stuart has organized *Feeding the 5000* events in more than 20 countries.

FINISH

START

If I make a strawberry smoothie, …

If we learn more about food waste, …

You left your fridge door open. Your food rotted. **GO BACK TO START.**

…, we get really sick.

You just used old bananas to make muffins! Great idea. **MOVE AHEAD THREE SPACES.**

If we reduce our food waste, …

…, share it with a friend.

…, we'll decrease the amount of food we waste.

If you make a sandwich for me, …

If you enjoy cooking, …

…, I usually throw it away.

…, it tastes awful.

…, don't buy them!

You just dropped your lunch and now you can't eat it. **LOSE A TURN.**

Plumber Stepanych

Release

Release

· Sculpture of Nelson Mandela
· 50 tall steel columns
· Columns are 6.5–9.5 m (21–31 ft.) tall
· Artist: Marco Cianfanelli
· Location: Howick, South Africa

Plumber Stepanych

· Built in 1998
· Life-size
· It's believed that hugging the statue will help you avoid plumbing problems.
· Artists: S. N. Noryshev and I. A. Vakhitov
· Location: Omsk, Russia

Rubber Duck

Federation Bells

Rubber Duck

· Several different versions of this sculpture
· This *Rubber Duck*: 22 m (72 ft.) tall and 20 m (65 ft.) wide
· Artist: Florentijn Hofman
· Traveled to cities around the world

Federation Bells

· 39 bells on tall poles
· Bells are between 2–6 m (6.5–30 ft.) tall
· Each bell plays a different note.
· Artists: Anton Hassell and Neil McLachlan
· Location: Melbourne, Australia

Before I Die

Jelly Baby Family

Jelly Baby Family

· Seven brightly colored figures
· Daddy Jelly Baby is 1.9 m (6 ft.) tall, weighs 350 kg (770 lb.)
· Also a mother and three children
· Artist: Mauro Perucchetti
· Location: Singapore

Before I Die

· Wall with chalkboard paint
· People can write their own wishes.
· Original wall: 12.5 m (41 ft.) wide, 2.5 m (8 ft.) tall
· Artist: Candy Chang
· Many different walls in different places

Photo

Photo

Information

Information

Photo

Photo

Information

Information

Photo

Photo

Information

Information

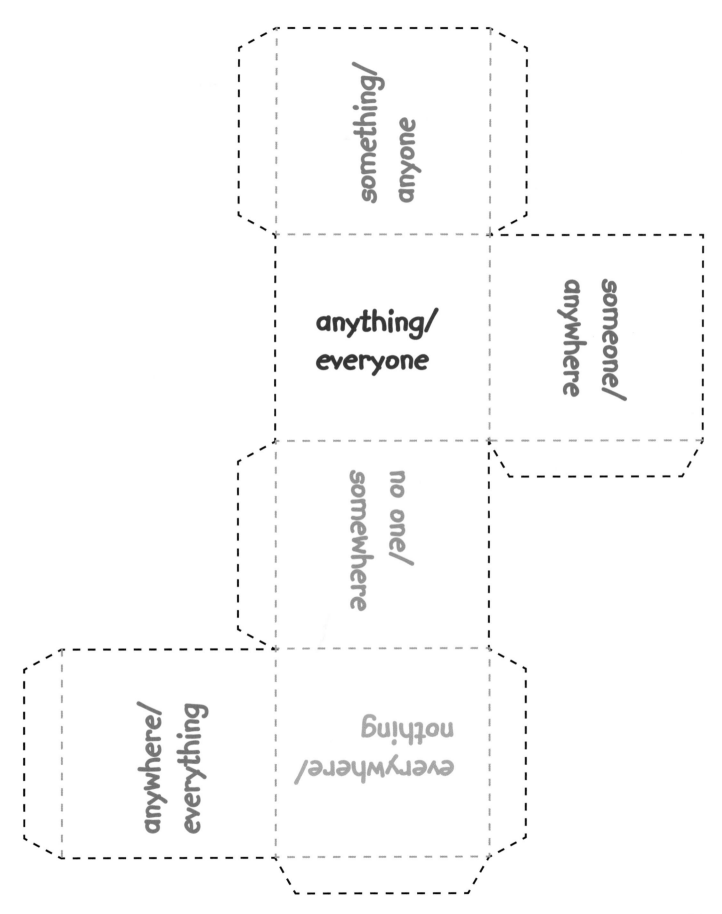

Did I ever tell you about . . . ? → **a volcanic eruption** → You didn't put out your campfire. **GO BACK TO START.**

↓

an avalanche ← **an earthquake** ← **a heat wave**

↓

You've prepared your emergency plan. **MOVE AHEAD TWO.** → **a blizzard** → **a flood**

↓

a wildfire ← You didn't listen to the severe weather warnings. **LOSE A TURN.** ← **a tornado**

↓

a cyclone → **lightning** → **YOU'RE SAFE!**

CONGRATULATIONS.

be / awake
today

live / in your
house

sit / in this
classroom

like /
favorite band

read /
this page

practice /
favorite pastime

learn / English

play /
(sport or musical
instrument)

have / favorite
item of clothing

know /
best friend